LEARN SPANISH IN 7 DAYS

The Ultimate Crash Course to Learning the Basics of the Spanish Language in No Time

By Dagny Taggart

© Copyright 2015

All rights reserved. No portion of this book may be reproduced - mechanically, electronically, or by any other means, including photocopying- without the permission of the publisher.

Disclaimer

The information provided in this book is designed to provide helpful information on the subjects discussed. The author's books are only meant to provide the reader with the basics knowledge of a certain language, without any warranties regarding whether the student will, or will not, be able to incorporate and apply all the information provided. Although the writer will make her best effort share her insights, language learning is a difficult task, and each person needs a different timeframe to fully incorporate a new language. This book, nor any of the author's books constitute a promise that the reader will learn a certain language within a certain timeframe.

Table of Contents

MY FREE GIFT TO YOU! 6

>> GET THE FULL SPANISH ONLINE COURSE WITH AUDIO LESSONS << 7

INTRODUCTION: ARE YOU READY FOR AN AMAZING JOURNEY? 8

SECTION 1: THE BASICS 12
- CHAPTER 1: GETTING THE PRONUNCIATION DOWN 13
- CHAPTER 2: SPANISH/ENGLISH DIFFERENCES - BASIC GRAMMAR 16
- CHAPTER 3: GREETINGS, INTRODUCTIONS, AND OTHER USEFUL PHRASES 22
- CHAPTER 4: ABOUT TIME - TELLING TIME, DAYS OF WEEK, DATES 28
- CHAPTER 5: HOW DO YOU LIKE THIS WEATHER? 33

SECTION 2: IN THE CITY AND TRAVELLING 36
- CHAPTER 6: DIRECTIONS 37
- CHAPTER 7: SHOPPING 42
- CHAPTER 8: GOING OUT TO EAT 48
- CHAPTER 9: GOING TO THE DOCTOR 54
- CHAPTER 10: GOING TO THE BANK 60
- CHAPTER 11: TRANSPORTATION 63
- CHAPTER 12: FINDING A PLACE TO STAY 72

SECTION 3: GETTING TO KNOW EACH OTHER 75
- CHAPTER 13: DESCRIBING PEOPLE & THINGS 76
- CHAPTER 14: WE ARE FAMILY! 83
- CHAPTER 15: ALL WORK AND NO PLAY? 88
- CHAPTER 16: HOBBIES 92

SECTION 4: GRAMMAR SCHOOL 96
- CHAPTER 17: TO BE OR NOT TO BE... THAT'S THE QUESTION! 97
- CHAPTER 18: "POR" Y "PARA" 102
- CHAPTER 19: CONJUGATING REGULAR VERBS IN THE PRESENT 105
- CHAPTER 20: TENER O NO TENER..113
- CONCLUSION: AREN'T YOU EXCITED? YOUR JOURNEY IS ABOUT TO BEGIN!...........117

>> GET THE FULL SPANISH ONLINE COURSE WITH AUDIO LESSONS << .118

PS: CAN I ASK YOU A QUICK FAVOR? 119

PREVIEW OF "SPANISH *FOR TOURISTS - THE MOST ESSENTIAL SPANISH GUIDE TO TRAVEL ABROAD, MEET PEOPLE & FIND YOUR WAY AROUND - ALL WHILE SPEAKING PERFECT SPANISH!"*..120

CHECK OUT MY OTHER BOOKS..133

ABOUT THE AUTHOR 134

Dedicated to those who love going beyond their own frontiers.

Keep on traveling,

Dagny Taggart

My FREE Gift to You!

As a way of saying thank you for downloading my book, I'd like to send you an exclusive gift that will revolutionize the way you learn new languages. It's an extremely comprehensive PDF with 15 language hacking rules that **will help you learn 300% faster, with less effort, and with higher than ever retention rates**.

This guide is an amazing complement to the book you just got, and could easily be a stand-alone product, but for now I've decided to give it away for free, to thank you for being such an awesome reader, and to make sure I give you all the value that I can to help you succeed faster on your language learning journey.

To get your FREE gift, go to the link below, write down your email address and I'll send it right away!

>> http://bit.ly/SpanishGift<<

GET INSTANT ACCESS

>> Get The Full Spanish Online Course With Audio Lessons <<

If you truly want to learn Spanish 300% FASTER, then hear this out.

I've partnered with the most revolutionary language teachers to bring you the very best Spanish online course I've ever seen. It's a mind-blowing program specifically created for language hackers such as ourselves. It will allow you learn Spanish 3x faster, straight from the comfort of your own home, office, or wherever you may be. It's like having an unfair advantage!

The Online Course consists of:

+ 185 Built-In Lessons
+ 98 Interactive Audio Lessons
+ 24/7 Support to Keep You Going

The program is extremely engaging, fun, and easy-going. You won't even notice you are learning a complex foreign language from scratch. And before you realize it, by the time you go through all the lessons you will officially become a truly solid Spanish speaker.

Old classrooms are a thing of the past. It's time for a language revolution.

If you'd like to go the extra mile, follow the link below and let the revolution begin

>> http://www.bitly.com/Spanish-Course <<

CHECK OUT THE COURSE »

Introduction
Are You Ready for an Amazing Journey?

Most people are daunted by the idea of learning a language. They think it's impossible, even unfathomable. I remember as a junior in high school, watching footage of Jackie O giving a speech in French. I was so impressed and inspired by the ease at which she spoke this other language of which I could not understand one single word.

At that moment, I knew I had to learn at least one foreign language. I started with Spanish, later took on Mandarin, and most recently have started learning Portuguese. No matter how challenging and unattainable it may seem, millions of people have done it. You do NOT have to be a genius to learn another language. You DO have to be willing to take risks and make mistakes, sometimes even make a fool of yourself, be dedicated, and of course, practice, practice, practice!

This book will only provide you with the basics in order to get started learning the Spanish language. It is geared towards those who are planning to travel to a Spanish-speaking country and covers many common scenarios you may find yourself in so feel free to skip around to the topic that is most prudent to you at the moment. It is also focused on the Spanish of Latin America rather than Spain. Keep in mind, every Spanish-speaking country has some language details specific to them so it would be essential to do some research on the specific country or countries that you will visit.

I will now list some tips that I have found useful and should be very helpful to you in your journey of learning Spanish. I don't wish you luck because that will not get you anywhere- reading this book, dedicating yourself, and taking some risks will!

Important note

Due to the nature of this book (it contains charts, graphs, and so on), you will better your reading experience by setting your device on *LANDSCAPE* mode!

Language Tips

Tip #1 - Keep an Open Mind

It may seem obvious but you must understand that languages are very different from each other. You cannot expect them to translate word for word. *'There is a black dog'* will not translate word for word with the same word order in Spanish. You have to get used to the idea of translating WHOLE ideas. So don't find yourself saying, *"Why is everything backwards in Spanish?"* because it may seem that way many times. Keep your mind open to the many differences that you will find in the language that go far beyond just the words.

Tip #2 - Take Risks

Be fearless. Talk to as many people as you can. The more practice you get the better and don't worry about looking like a fool when you say, *"I am pregnant"* rather than *"I am embarrassed,"* which as you will find out can be a common mistake. If anyone is laughing remember they are not laughing at you. Just laugh with them, move on, and LEARN from it, which brings us to our next tip.

Tip #3 - Learn from your Mistakes

It doesn't help to get down because you made one more mistake when trying to order at a restaurant, take a taxi, or just in a friendly conversation. Making mistakes is a HUGE part of learning a language. You have to put yourself out there as we said and be willing to make tons of mistakes! Why? Because what can you do with mistakes. You can LEARN from them. If you never make a mistake, you probably are not learning as much as you could. So every time you mess up when trying to communicate, learn from it, move on, and keep your head up!

Tip #4 - Immerse yourself in the language

If you're not yet able to go to a Spanish-speaking country, try to pretend that you are. Surround yourself with Spanish. Listen to music in Spanish, watch movies, TV shows, in Spanish. Play games on your phone, computer, etc. in Spanish. Another great idea is to actually put your phone, computer, tablet and/or other electronic devices in Spanish. It can be frustrating at first but in the end this exposure will definitely pay off.

Tip #5 - Start Thinking in Spanish

I remember being a senior in high school and working as a lifeguard at a fairly deserted pool. While I was sitting and staring at the empty waters, I would speak to myself or think to myself (to not seem so crazy) in Spanish. I would describe my surroundings, talk about what I had done and what I was going to do, etc. While I was riding my bike, I would do the same thing. During any activity when you don't need to talk or think about anything else, keep your brain constantly going in Spanish to get even more practice in the language. So get ready to turn off the English and jumpstart your Spanish brain!

Tip #6 - Label your Surroundings/Use Flashcards

When I started to learn Portuguese, I bought an excellent book that included stickers so that you could label your surroundings. So I had stickers all over my parents' house from the kitchen to the bathroom that labeled the door, the dishes, furniture, parts of the house, etc. It was a great, constant reminder of how to say these objects in another language. You can just make your own labels and stick them all over the house and hope it doesn't bother your family or housemates too much!

Tip #7 - Use Context clues, visuals, gestures, expressions, etc.

If you don't understand a word that you have heard or read, look or listen to the surrounding words and the situation to help you. If you are in a restaurant and your friend says, "I am going to ??? a sandwich." You can take a guess that she said *order* or *eat* but you don't have to understand every word in order to understand the general meaning. When you are in a conversation use gestures, expressions, and things around you to help communicate your meaning. Teaching English as a second language to young learners taught me this. If you act everything out, you are more likely to get your point across. If you need to say the word *bird* and you don't know how you can start flapping your arms and chirping and then you will get your point across and possibly learn how to say *bird*. It may seem ridiculous but as I said, you have to be willing to look silly to learn another language and this greatly helps your language communication and learning.

Tip #8 - Circumlocution

Circumlo... what? This is just a fancy word for describing something when you don't know how to say it. If you are looking to buy an umbrella and don't know how to say it, what can you do? You can describe it using words you know. You can say, it is something used for the rain that opens and closes and then hopefully someone will understand you, help you, and maybe teach you how to say this word. Using circumlocution is excellent language practice and is much better than just giving up when you don't know how to say a word. So keep talking even if you have a limited vocabulary. Say what you can and describe or act out what you can't!

SECTION 1: THE BASICS

Chapter 1
Getting the Pronunciation Down

Below I will break down general Spanish pronunciation for the whole alphabet dividing it into vowels and consonants. One great thing about Spanish is that the letters almost always stay consistent as far as what sound they make. Unlike English in which the vowels can make up to 27 different sounds depending on how they are mixed. Be thankful that you don't have to learn English or at least have already learned English. There are of course some sounds in Spanish that we never make in English and you possibly have never made in your life. So get ready to start moving your mouth and tongue in a new way that may seem strange at first but as I keep saying, practice makes perfect!

The charts on the next page will explain how to say the letter, pronounce it, and if there is an example in an English word of how to say it I put it in the right column.

Vowel Sounds

Vowel	How to say the letter	How to pronounce it in a word	As in…
a	Ah	Ah	T<u>a</u>co
e	A	A	<u>A</u>ce
i	Ee	Ee	<u>Ea</u>sy
o	Oh	Oh	<u>O</u>pen
u	Oo	Oo	B<u>oo</u>k

Consonant Sounds

Consonant	How to say the letter	How to pronounce it in a word	As in…
b	beh	similar to English b	

c	<u>c</u>eh	k after *a, o,* or *u* s after *e* or *i*	<u>c</u>at <u>c</u>ereal
ch	<u>ch</u>eh	ch	<u>ch</u>eese
d	<u>d</u>eh	a soft d (place your tongue at the back of your upper teeth)	th<u>r</u>ee
f	e<u>f</u>e	F	<u>f</u>ree
g	<u>g</u>eh	h before i or e g before a, o, u	<u>h</u>im <u>g</u>o
h	<u>a</u>che	silent	
j	<u>h</u>ota	H	<u>h</u>im
k	<u>k</u>ah	K	<u>k</u>araoke
l	e<u>l</u>e	like English l with tongue raised to roof of mouth	
ll	e<u>y</u>e	Y	<u>y</u>es
m	e<u>m</u>e	M	<u>m</u>oney
n	e<u>n</u>e	N	<u>n</u>o
ñ	e<u>ny</u>e	Ny	can<u>y</u>on
p	<u>p</u>eh	like English p but you don't aspirate	

Consonants continued

Consonant	How to say the letter	How to pronounce it in a word	As in...
Q	<u>koo</u>	k (q is always followed by u but the u is silent) Ex: quemar = kaymar	<u>k</u>ill
R	<u>ere</u>	* at the beginning of a word you must roll your r's by vibrating tongue at roof of	

		mouth * in the middle of a word it sounds like a soft d	
rr	erre	roll your r's as mentioned above	
S	ese	Like English s	sorry
T	teh	a soft English t, the tongue touches the back of the upper teeth	
V	veh	like Spanish b	boots

Consonants continued

Consonant	How to say the letter	How to pronounce it in a word	As in…
w	dobleveh	like English w	water
x	equis	*Between vowels and at the end of a word, it sounds like the English *ks*. *At the beginning of a word, it sounds like the letter *s*.	*box *sorry
y	igriega	like English y	yellow
z	seta	s	six

Note: If you're not sure how to pronounce a word, one thing you can do is type it in *Google translate* then click on the little speaker icon in the bottom left corner to hear the correct pronunciation.

Chapter 2
Spanish/English Differences - Basic Grammar

We will now start with the most basic. I will explain some major things that are different between English and Spanish and some general Spanish grammar rules. Along with this, I will include basic vocabulary such as question words, numbers, colors, and other useful words and phrases to give you a foundation to help support you through the rest of this book. If you are trying to answer the practice questions in the following chapters and don't know how to say a vocabulary word, you will most likely find it in this chapter.

Differences between English and Spanish

1. **Masculine and Feminine Words:** In Spanish there are words that are feminine and masculine. It has nothing to do with the actual word. For example the word *dress* ("el vestido") is masculine and the word *beard* ("la barba") is feminine.

2. **Word Order:** The word order is often changed. For example, the adjective goes after the noun. Instead of the *red car*, it is the *car red* ("carro rojo").

3. **Adjective and Noun Agreement:** The adjectives must agree with the gender (feminine or masculine) and the number (singular or plural). For example, the red cars ("los carros rojos") or the black cat ("la gata negra")

4. **Verb Changes**: Spanish has more verb changes the verb run changes 5 times in the present tense. I run (corro) you run (corres) he or she runs (corre) we run (corremos) they or you all run (corren). For this reason, Spanish also uses personal pronouns much less as I will mention in number 5.

5. **Lack of Pronoun (I, he, she, we, it, they, etc.) Use:** Because of the verb changes mentioned in number 4, you do not have to use pronouns as often. Instead of saying *tú corres,*(you run) you can just say *corres* because we already know that is you who we are talking about from the verb.

6. **Formal You:** There is a formal way to say *you* ("Usted" usually written Ud.) that is used to show respect to your elders or those in a higher position than you or simply for those whom you don't know well. I used this form throughout most of the book because you can safely use it with anyone.

7. **Word Endings:** Diminutives are very commonly added to words especially the diminutive 'ito' which is used to say something in a cuter way or to talk about something that is a small. For example, "the cute little dog" (el perrito) but it is used much more frequently than in English and can be added to adjectives and nouns.

8. **Lack of Capitalization:** Many words that are capitalized in English are not in Spanish. For example, days of the week, months, languages and nationalities.

Ex: Tuesday = el martes
February = febrero
Spanish = español
Canadian = canadiense

Basic Grammar

There are four ways to say *the* in Spanish listed below

Spanish Articles

The	Masculine	Feminine
Singular	El	La
Plural	Los	Las

Note: 'El,' 'la,' 'los,' and 'las' all mean 'the' in English.

Ex: *el* gato ---> the cat

la persona ---> the person

los perros ---> the dogs

las guitarras ---> the guitars

Note: The articles are used much more frequently in Spanish.

Ex: I like apples ---> Me gustan las manzanas.

Personal Pronouns

I	yo
you	tú
he, she, you (formal)	él, ella, Usted (Ud.)
We	Nosotros (masculine) Nosotras (feminine)
They, you all	Ellos (masculine), Ellas (feminine), Ustedes (Uds.)

*As mentioned before, personal pronouns are not used as much in Spanish

Question Words

What?	¿Qué?
Where?	¿Dónde?
When?	¿Cuándo?
Which?	¿Cuál?
Why?	¿Por qué?
Who?	¿Quién?

Numbers 1-10

1	uno
2	dos
3	tres
4	cuatro
5	cinco
6	seis
7	siete
8	ocho
9	nueve
10	diez

Numbers 11-20

11	once
12	doce
13	trece
14	catorce
15	quince
16	dieciseis
17	diecisiete
18	dieciocho
19	diecinueve
20	veinte

Note: From 16-19 you basically just say 10 and 6 (dieciseis) 10 and 7 (diecisiete), etc.

*For 21-29 it follows this pattern: veinti + number as one word

Ex: 21 ---> veintiuno, 22 ---> veintidos, 23 ---> veintitres, etc.

Numbers 30-100+

30	treinta
40	cuarenta
50	cincuenta
60	sesenta
70	setenta
80	ochenta
90	noventa
100	cien
105	ciento cinco
115	ciento quince

*For 31-99 it follows this pattern: treinta + number as two separate words   **Ex:**   33   =   treinta y tres

45   =   cuarenta y cinco

78   =   setente y ocho,

* For 101 to 199, just say ciento + the number
Ex: 190= ciento noventa (see examples above)

Numbers 200-1000

200	doscientos
300	trescientos
400	cuatrocientos
500	**quinientos**
600	seiscientos
700	**setecientos**
800	ochocientos
900	**novecientos**
1000	mil

* Notice how the pattern changes with the numbers in bold

Colors

Red	Rojo/a
Orange	Anaranjado/a
Yellow	Amarillo/a
Green	Verde
Blue	Azúl
Purple	Morado/a
Pink	Rosado/a
Black	Negro/a
White	Blanco/a
Brown	Marrón
Gray	Gris

Other useful vocabulary and phrases

Yes	sí
No	no
But	pero
also/too	también
Is	es (permanent) / está (temporary)

And	y
An	un (masculine) una (feminine)
In	en
With	con
Or	o
Now	ahora
because	porque
Well	pues/bueno
Sorry	lo siento
excuse me	perdón
thank you	gracias
you're welcome	de nada
Please	por favor
me too.	yo también
Very	Muy
A lot	Mucho
That's okay/Okay	Está bien.

Chapter 3
Greetings, Introductions, and Other Useful Phrases

¿Cómo está Ud.?

In this chapter we will go over the very necessary ways to greet and introduce yourself to others. We have to remember that there are two different ways of saying *you* in Spanish- the formal (Ud.) and the informal (tú). I remember often worrying about when to use one or the other. If you are unsure you can just go with Ud. to stay safe. Below is a list of common greetings in Spanish.

Common Greetings

Hello	Hola
Good Morning	Buenos Días
Good Afternoon	Buenas Tardes
Good evening/Good night	Buenas Noches
General Greeting	Buenas (People often just shorten it for a general greeting)

Asking and Answering 'How are you?'

How are you? (informal)	¿Cómo estás?
How are you? (formal)	¿Cómo está Ud.?
How are you doing? (informal)	¿Cómo te va?
How are you doing? (formal)	¿Cómo le va?
How are you?	¿Qué tal?
Well/Very well	Bien/Muy bien
Good and you? (informal)	¿Bien y tú?
Good and you? (formal)	¿Bien y Ud?
So-so	Así así
What's up? What's new?	¿Qué hay?

Saying Goodbye

English	Spanish
Goodbye	Adiós
See you later	Hasta luego

See you tomorrow	Hasta mañana
See you soon	Hasta pronto
See you	Nos vemos
Bye	Chau

¡Práctica!

Translate the following conversation into English

#1

- ¡Hola Pedro! ----->

- ¡Buenos días Ana! ----->

- ¿Cómo te va? ----->

- Muy bien, gracias, ¿y Ud.? ----->

- Excelente, gracias. ----->

- Hasta luego, Ana. ----->

- ¡Nos vemos, Pedro! ----->

*Did you notice there were some words that were not listed in the vocabulary above? Were you still able to use context clues and/or cognates (words that sound similar in both languages) and fill in the rest of the meaning as is suggested in the introduction? Remember, it is a great skill to have because most of the time there will be words that you may not understand in a conversation.

Introductions and Other phrases

What is your name? (informal)	¿Cómo te llamas?
What is your name? (formal)	¿Cómo se llama?
My name is…	Me llamo…
Nice to meet you!	¡Mucho gusto!
It's a pleasure.	Es un placer.
Me too.	Yo también

Where are you from?	¿De dónde eres?
I am from the U.S.	Soy de los estados unidos.
How old are you?	¿Cuántos años tiene?
I am... years old.	Tengo ... años.
Canada	Cánada
England	Inglaterra
South Africa	África del Sur
Australia	Australia

Cultural Note: **Kissing** ---In Spanish speaking countries, people usually greet with a kiss on one cheek, or both cheeks (in Spain)

*Below, I will list some useful phrases for when you don't understand, are confused, and need some clarification: a very common occurrence when learning a language.

Other Useful Phrases

I don't understand.	No entiendo.
Can you repeat, please.	¿Puede repetir, por favor?
Speak more slowly, please.	Hable más despacio, por favor.
How do you say ...?	¿Cómo se dice...?
What does this mean?	¿Qué significa esto?
What is this?	¿Qué es esto?
Can you help me?	¿Me puede ayudar?
Do you speak English?	¿Habla inglés?
I speak a little Spanish.	Hablo un poco de español.
I don't know.	No sé.
Write it down, please.	Escríbalo por favor.

¡La Práctica!

Translate the following conversation into English

#2

- ¡Buenas tardes! ----->

- ¡Buenas! ¿Cómo está Ud? ----->

- Bien, gracias, ¿y tú? ----->

- Así así, gracias. ----->

- ¿Cómo se llama Ud.? ----->

- Me llamo Adriana, ¿y tú cómo te llamas? ----->

- Me llamo Alberto. ----->

- ¿Cuántos años tiene? ----->

- Tengo 25 años y tú? ----->

- Tengo 29 años. ¿De dónde eres? ----->

- Soy de Canadá. ¿De dónde eres tú? ----->

- Soy de Colombia. ----->

- ¡Mucho gusto! ----->

- ¡Es un placer para mí también! ----->

Match the Phrases
1. I speak a little Spanish----------------------------a. ¿Qué es esto?
2. Write it down, please. ----------------------------b. No entiendo
3. Do you speak English? ---------------------------c. Hablo un poco de español.
4. I don't understand. ------------------------------d. No sé
5. How do you say...?------------------------------e. Hable màs despacio por favor.
6. I don't know. ------------------------------------f. ¿Qué significa esto?
7. Speak slowly please. ---------------------------g. Escríbalo por favor.
8. Can you repeat, please? ------------------------h. ¿Habla inglés?
9. What is this? ------------------------------------i. ¿Còmo se dice...?
10. What does this mean? -------------------------j. ¿Puede repetir, por favor?

Chapter 3 Answers

Translation #1

- ¡Hola Pedro!
- ¡Buenos días Ana!
- ¿Cómo te va?
- Muy bien, gracias, ¿y Ud.?
- Excelente, gracias.
- Hasta luego, Ana.
- ¡Nos vemos, Pedro!

- Hi Pedro!
- Good morning, Ana!
- How's it going?
- Very good, thanks. And you?
- Excellent, thanks.
- See you later, Ana.
- See you, Pedro!

Translation #2

- ¡Buenas tardes!
- ¡Buenas! ¿Cómo está Ud?
- Bien, gracias, ¿y tú?
- Así así, gracias.
- ¿Cómo se llama Ud.?
- Me llamo Adriana, ¿y tú cómo te llamas?
- Me llamo Alberto.
- ¿Cuántos años tiene?
- Tengo 25 años y tú?
- Tengo 29 años. ¿De dónde eres?
- Soy de Canadá. ¿De dónde eres tú?
- Soy de Colombia.
- Es un placer conocerlo.
- ¡Es un placer para mí también

- Good afternoon!
- Hi! How are you?
- Good, thanks. And you?

- So so, thank you.
- What's your name?
- My name is Adriana, And you what is your name?
- My name is Alberto.
- How old are you?
- I am 25 years old and you?
- I'm 29 years old. Where are you from?
- I am from Canada. Where are you from?
- I am from Colombia
- Nice to meet you!
- It's a pleasure for me too!

Match the Phrases
1. I speak a little Spanish. -----------c. Hablo un poco de español
2. Write it down, please. ------------g. Escríbalo por favor.
3. Do you speak English?   -----------h. ¿Habla inglés?
4. I don't understand. ---------------b. No entiendo.
5. How do you say…?----------------i. ¿Còmo se dice…?
6. I don't know. ----------------------d. No sé.
7. Speak slowly please.--------------e. Hable màs despacio por favor.
8. Can you repeat, please?---------j. ¿Puede repetir, por favor?
9. What is this?----------------------a. ¿Qué es esto
10. What does this mean? ----------f. ¿Qué significa esto?

Chapter 4
About Time - Telling time, Days of Week, Dates

In this chapter, I will discuss how to talk about time, telling time, days of week, months, etc. Something to remember about Latin-American cultures is that time is much more relaxed. When you are invited to a gathering with friends, it is acceptable to show up a couple of hours late. I remember when I studied in Chile, most of the students who showed up to class on time, were foreigners. The Chilean students usually would file in 15 to 30 minutes late. I also recall going to an interview in the Dominican Republic and showing up 15 minutes early as one should. I ended up waiting for over an hour until the interview started. Typically with business and school, time is stricter, but not always as my experience has taught me. Below I have several useful phrases to talk about time.

Telling Time

What time is is?	¿Qué hora es?
It's one.	Es la una.
It's two.	Son las dos… (*Son las* is used for times 2-12)
It's four thirty.	Son las cuatro y media.
It's fifteen until eight.	Son las ocho menos quince.
a.m. (in the morning)	de la mañana
p.m. (in the afternoon)	de la tarde
p.m. (at night)	de la noche

* If you want to add minutes to the hour just use the word 'y'

Ex: It is 6:05   =   Son las seis y cinco

Now you try:

1. It is 3:05 _____

2. It is 10:45 _____

3. It is 8:20 _____

*If you want to say that it is 15 til, 10 til, or 5 til an hour, use the following format:

It is five minus ten (It is ten til five) = Son las cinco menos diez

Now you try:

4. It is fifteen til three_____
5. It is five til seven _____
6. It is ten til nine_____

Days of the Week

What day is today? Today is Thursday	¿Qué día es hoy? Hoy es jueves
Today	Hoy
Yesterday	Ayer
Tomorrow	Mañana
Monday	el lunes
Tuesday	el martes
Wednesday	el miércoles
Thursday	el jueves
Friday	el viernes
Saturday	el sábado
Sunday	el domingo

* As mentioned before, Spanish does not typically capitalize the days of the weeks.

* Also, when you are saying *On Monday I'm going to the doctor* > *El lunes voy al doctor* (you only said the day of the week with *el* and not *on*)

Talking about the Date

What is the date today?	¿Cuál es la fecha hoy?
Today is February 15th	Hoy es el quince de febrero
January	enero
February	febrero

March	marzo
April	abril
May	mayo
June	junio
July	julio
August	agosto
September	septiembre
October	octubre
November	noviembre
December	diciembre

*Date format

Es el <u>day (#)</u> de <u>month</u>

Es el <u>quince</u> de <u>junio.</u> = It is June 15th

¡La Práctica!

Choose the correct answer

7. ¿Qué hora es?

a. Son el uno de la tarde ----------------------b. Es la una de la tarde

c. Son la una de la tarde ----------------------- d. Es el uno de la tarde

8. **Hoy es jueves.**

a. Today is Monday ---------------------- b. Today is Friday

c. Today is Sunday ---------------------- d. Today is Thursday.

9. **Today is March 27th**

a. Hoy es el 27 de marzo ---------------------- b. Hoy es marzo 27

c. Hoy es 27 de marzo ---------------------- d. Hoy es el 27 marzo

10. **It is ten til seven**

a. Son las menos siete diez ---------------------- b. Son las siete menos diez

c. Son la siete menos diez ---------------------- d. Son las diez menos siete

11. It is 3:15?

a. Es las tres y quince ---------------------- b. Son la tres quince

c. Son las tres y quince ---------------------- d. Es la tres y quince

Chapter 4 Answers

1. It is 3:05 ----> Son las tres y cinco.

2. It is 10:45 ----> Son las diez cuarenta y cinco or Son las once menos quince.

3. It is 8:20 ----> Son las ocho y veinte.

4. It is fifteen til three. ----> Son las tres menos quince.

5. It is five til seven. ----> Son las siete menos cinco.

6. It is ten til nine. ----> Son las nueve menos diez.

Choose the correct answer

7. ¿Qué hora es?

b. Es la una de la tarde

8. Hoy es jueves.

d. Today is Thursday.

9. Today is March 27th

a. Hoy es el 27 de marzo

10. It is ten til seven

b. Son las siete menos diez

11. It is 3:15?

c. Son las tres y quince

Chapter 5
How Do You Like This Weather?

¿Qué tiempo hace?

This chapter will discuss how to talk about the weather, something people often talk about when there is nothing else to talk about. It also is useful information to have, as in some Spanish-speaking countries, it can be perfectly sunny one moment and then torrentially raining, the next. When asking how the weather is, you will learn about some expressions using the word 'hace' which actually means 'does or makes.' So you are literally asking 'What the weather does?' and answering 'it makes sunny,' 'it does windy,' etc when of course the actual meaning is *'it is windy.'* Another reminder that languages rarely will translate word for word. Below are some useful phrases and vocabulary to use when talking about the weather.

Weather Expressions

What's the weather like today?	¿Qué tiempo hace hoy? or ¿Cómo está el tiempo hoy?
It is cold	Hace frío
It is hot	Hace calor
It is sunny	Hace sol
It is windy	Hace viento
The weather is nice	Hace buen tiempo
The weather is bad	Hace mal tiempo
It's cool.	Hace fresco
It's raining.	Está lloviendo
Is it going to rain today?	¿Va a llover hoy?
Yes, it's going to rain, No, it's not going to rain	Sí va a llover/No, no va a llover
It's snowing	Está nevando
Really?	¿De veras?

* If you want to say: It is very hot, cold, etc. you must use *mucho* NOT *muy*

Ex: It is very hot ---->Hace mucho calor

It is very cold ----> Hace mucho frío, etc.

¡La Práctica!

Choose the correct answer

1. ¿Qué tiempo hace hoy?

a. Es mucho calor -----------------b. Está mucho calor

c. Hace mucho calor ----------------- d. Hace muy calor

2. It is very sunny today.

a. Hace mucho sol hoy ----------------- b. Es mucho sol hoy.

c. Hace muy sol hoy. ----------------- d. Está muy sol hoy.

3. ¿Va a llover hoy?

a. No, no llover hoy ----------------- b. Sí, va a llover hoy

c. Sí va hoy llover ----------------- d. No, no hoy va llover

Translate to Spanish

- Hi friend, how are you?

- Good! How is the weather today?

- It's nice! It's not going to rain.

- But, it is very windy.

- Yes, but very sunny too.

- See you tomorrow!

- Goodbye!

Chapter 5 Answers

Choose the correct answer

1. ¿Qué tiempo hace hoy?

c. Hace mucho calor

2. It is very sunny today.

a. Hace mucho sol hoy

3. ¿Va a llover hoy?

b. Sí, va a llover hoy

Translation

- Hi friend, how are you?
- Good! How is the weather today?
- It's nice! It's not going to rain.
- But, it is very windy.
- Yes, but very sunny too.
- See you tomorrow!
- Goodbye!

- Hola amigo/amiga, ¿cómo estás?
- ¡Bien! ¿Qué tiempo hace hoy?
- ¡Hace buen tiempo! No va a llover.
- Pero, hace mucho viento.
- Si, pero hace mucho sol también.
- Hasta mañana!
- ¡Adios!

SECTION 2
IN THE CITY AND TRAVELLING

Chapter 6
Directions

¿Dónde está el banco?

Now, we will move onto some more very useful everyday vocabulary, especially if you are in a new country and have no idea where anything is. Now, these days with google maps and GPS, stopping to ask for directions is less common. However, in many Spanish-speaking countries, you will not have such easy access to internet while you are on the streets at least. So get ready to have to actually talk to people face to face and maybe occasionally get a little lost. Below I have some of the most useful phrases and vocabulary for getting around in Spanish.

Phrases to talk about Directions

Where is it?	¿Donde está?
Excuse me, where is the…	¿Perdón dónde está el/la …?
It's next to the…	Está al lado de la/del …
It's in front of the…	Está al frente de la/ del …
Keep straight	Sigue derecho
Turn right	Dobla a la derecha
Turn left	Dobla a la izquierda
It's on the right/left	Está a la derecha/ a la izquierda
Far from	Lejos de
Near to	Cerca de
Above	Encima de
Below	Abajo de
Behind	Atrás de

* Notice the contraction:

de + el = del

de + la = de la (stays the same)

Places

The bank	El banco
The restaurant	El restaurante
The post office	El correo
The supermarket	El supermercado

The pharmacy	La farmacia
The bakery	La panadería
Bus/Train station	Estación del Bus/Tren
Store	Tienda
Church	Iglesia
Stationary Store	Papelería

*Did you notice which words are masculine and feminine?

Notice the difference: It is next to the bank = Está al lado **del** banco.

It is next to the store = Está al lado **de la** tienda.

Other Phrases

I am lost.	Estoy perdido/perdida
How do I get to …?	¿Cómo llego a …?
Cross the street.	Cruza la calle.
Where am I now?	¿Dónde estoy ahora?
the corner	la esquina
one block	una cuadra
street	calle
here	aquí
there	ahí/allí
there	allá (farther away)

Time Expressions

Before	Antes
Now	Ahora
After	Después
Later/Then	Luego

¡La Práctica!

Choose the correct answer

1. The bank is next to the post office.

a. El banco está al lado de el correo.----- b. El banco es al lado del correo.

c. El banco está al lado de la correo. .----- d. El banco está al lado del correo.

2. Turn right at the bakery.

a. Dobla la derecha en la tienda.----- b. Dobla a la derecha en la panadería.

c. Dobla a la izquierda en la panadería. .----- d. Dobla a la derecha en la tienda.

3. The store is close to the church.

a. La tienda está cerca de la iglesia.   .----- b. La tienda está al frente del iglesia.

c. La tienda está lejos de la iglesia.   .----- d. La tienda es cerca de la iglesia.

Translate to English

- ¿Perdón, dónde está la estación de bus?

- Sigue derecho y dobla a la izquierda en la esquina.

- Ok.

- Despues, sigue por tres cuadras.

- Ok

- y cruza la calle y está al lado de la papelería.

- ¿Está muy lejos?

- No, no está muy lejos.

- ¡Pues, muchas gracias, señor!

- De nada, hasta luego.

Chapter 6 Answers

Choose the correct answer

1. The bank is next to the post office.

d. El banco está al lado del correo.

2. Turn right at the bakery.

b. Dobla a la derecha en la panadería.

3. The store is close to the church.
a. La tienda está cerca de la iglesia.

Translation

- ¿Perdón, dónde está la estación de bus?
- Sigue derecho y dobla a la izquierda en la esquina.
- Ok.
- Despues, sigue por tres cuadras.
- Ok
- y cruza la calle y está al lado de la papelería.
- ¿Está muy lejos?
- No, no está muy lejos.
- ¡Pues, muchas gracias, señor!
- De nada, hasta luego.

- Excuse me, where is the bus station?
- Keep straight and turn left at the corner y dobla a la izquierda en la esquina.
- Ok.
- Then, keep going for three blocks.
- Ok
- and cross the Street and it's next to the stationary store
- Is it very far?
- No, it's not very far.
- Well, thank you sir!
- Your welcome, see you later.

Chapter 7
Shopping

¿Cuánto cuesta eso?

Now, let's move onto a very enjoyable (usually) and common activity that we do in other countries- shopping! Whether it be shopping for cheesy souvenirs for your friends and family or shopping for some stylish local clothes for yourself, we've got the basics to help you bargain around and hopefully find what you are looking for. Remember that bargaining can be a big part of shopping in the markets of most Spanish-speaking countries. If you don't do it, you definitely will get taken advantage of by some lucky shopkeepers who see the 'gringo' coming from a mile away. So, let's see if we can find you a great deal!

Shopping phrases

How can I help you?	¿Cómo le puedo ayudar?
How much does it cost?	¿Cuánto cuesta?
How much is it?	¿Cuánto es?
Which one do you want?	¿Cuál quiere?
I would like that one.	Quisiera ese (masculine) esa (feminine)
It's too expensive	Está muy caro
Do you have…?	¿Tiene …?
Do you have bigger/smaller?	¿Tiene más grande/más pequeño?
Do you accept credit cards?	¿Acepta tarjetas de crédito?
We only accept cash.	Sólo aceptamos efectivo.
Can I try it on?	¿Puedo probármelo?
I'm just looking.	Sólo estoy mirando.
Of course!	¡Claro que sí!

Shopping Vocabulary

souvenirs	los recuerdos
clothes	la ropa
shirt	la camisa
pants	los pantalones
shorts	los shorts

a dress	un vestido
a jacket	una chaqueta
shoes	los zapatos
cap	el gorro
keychain	el llavero

* Note that you say *un/una* for *a* and it has to match the gender of the word.
Ex: un vestido = a dress
una camisa = a shirt

Below, I will list the demonstrative adjectives in Spanish (this, that, these, those) as they are very useful to use when shopping, 'I would like that one, please.'

Demonstrative Adjectives (This, That, These, Those)

*Note: These also change according to gender and number

This and That

English	Masculine	Feminine	Gender Neutral (When you don't know}
This	Este	Esta	Esto
That	Ese	Esa	Eso

These and Those

English	Masculine	Feminine
These	Estos	Estas
Those	Esos	Esas

* If you want to say: *that shirt*, remember to match 'that' to the word shirt.

Ex: es**a** chaquet**a** = that

es**e** gorr**o** = that

est**as** camis**as** = these

est**os** llaver**os** = these key chains

¡La Práctica!

Choose the correct answer

1. Camisetas

a. Esta .-----b. Estas

c. Este .-----d. Estos

2. I would like these shoes.

a. Quisiera esos zapatos. .----- b. Quisiera estas zapatos.

c. Quisiera estos zapatos. .----- d. Quisiera esas zapatos.

3. Would you like this jacket?

a. ¿Quisieras esta camiseta? .----- b. ¿Quisieras esta chaqueta?

c. ¿Quisiera este camiseta? .----- d. ¿Quisiera esa chaqueta?

Translate to English

- Buenos días, ¿Cómo le puedo ayudar?

- Sólo estoy mirando, gracias.

- De nada.

- ¿Cuánto cuesta este vestido?

- Doscientos pesos.

- ¡Está muy caro! ¿Y estos pantalones?

- Ciento cincuenta pesos.

- ¿Puedo probármelos?

- ¡Claro que sí!

- ¿Acepta tarjetas de crédito?

- No, sólo aceptamos efectivo.

  Está bien, muchas gracias.

Chapter 7 Answers

Choose the correct answer

1. Camisetas

b. Estas

2. I would like these shoes.

c. Quisiera estos zapatos.

3. Would you like this jacket?

b. ¿Quisieras esta chaqueta?

Translation

- Buenos días, ¿Cómo le puedo ayudar?
- Sólo estoy mirando, gracias.
- De nada.
- ¿Cuánto cuesta este vestido?
- Doscientos pesos.
- ¡Está muy caro! ¿Y estos pantalones?
- Ciento cincuenta pesos.
- ¿Puedo probármelos?
- ¡Claro que sí!
- ¿Acepta tarjetas de crédito?
- No, sólo aceptamos efectivo.
- Está bien, muchas gracias.
- Good morning, how can I help you?
- I'm just looking, thanks.
- Your welcome.
- How much does this dress cost?
- 200 pesos.
- It's very expensive! And these pants?
- 150 pesos.
- Can I try them on?
- Of course!
- Do you accept credit cards?

- No, we only accept cash.
- Okay, thank you very much.

Chapter 8
Going out to eat

Me gustaría comer...

In this chapter we will discuss another common and delicious activity- going out to eat in restaurants. Some cultural suggestions for going out to eat could be to not expect the same type of service that you get back home. The servers are not usually working as hard for their tips as they are in the U.S. Of course, every country is different. You also may have to specify if you want your water carbonated (con gas) or regular (sin gas) literally water with or without gas. Let's get ready to eat! Bon Appetite or as they say in Spanish, *Buen Provecho!*

Restaurant phrases

What can I bring you?	¿Qué le puedo traer?
I would like to eat...	Me gustaría comer...
I would like to drink...	Me gustaría beber...
Menu, please	El menú, por favor
What do you recommend?	¿Qué me recomienda?
Can you bring me?	Me puede traer...
Excuse me, sir	Perdón, señor
Excuse me, ma'am	Perdón, señora Perdon, señorita (younger)
La bebida	Drink
A glass	Un vaso
Soft Drink	Refresco
Juice	Jugo
A glass of water	Un vaso de agua
A beer	Una cerveza
A glass of wine	Un vaso de vino
Dessert	El postre
Tip	La propina
check, please	la cuenta, por favor
So/then	Entonces

Food Vocabulary

What does this dish have?	¿Qué tiene este plato?
Does this dish have…?	¿Este plato tiene …?
Meat	Carne
Fish	Pescado
Chicken	Pollo
Ham	Jamón
Egg	Huevo
Pasta	Pasta
Salad	Ensalada
Bread	Pan
Cheese	Queso
Vegetables	Verduras
Breakfast	Desayuno
Lunch	Almuerzo
Dinner	Cena
There is/there are	Hay

*A very useful verb, **Hay= There is/There are**, is pronounced like the letter I

Ex: Hay mucho pan y queso = There is a lot of bread and cheese.
Para almuerzo, hay sándwiches de jamón. =For lunch, there are ham sandwiches.

¡La Práctica!

Choose the correct answer

1. This dish has fish, vegetables, and bread.

a. Este plato tiene pescado, verduras, y pan

b. Esta plato tiene pescado, carne, y pan.

c. Este plato tiene queso, pollo, y pan.

d. Estos plato tiene pescado, jamón, y pan.

2. Can you bring me a beer please?

a. ¿Te puede traer una cerveza, por favor?

b. ¿Me puede traer un jugo, gracias?

c. ¿Me puede traer una cerveza, por favor?

d. ¿Le puede traer una cerveza, por favor?

3. Excuse me ma'am, the check please.

a. Perdon señor, la cuenta por favor.

b. Perdón señorita, el postre por favor.

c. Perdón señora, la propina por favor.

d. Perdón señorita, la cuenta por favor.

4. Para el desayuno, hay pan, queso, y huevos.

a. For lunch there is bread, cheese, and eggs.

b. For breakfast, there is fish, ham, and eggs.

c. For breakfast there is bread, cheese, and eggs.

d. For dinner there is ham, eggs, and bread.

5. Después de la cena, quisiera postre.

a. Before lunch, I would like dessert.
b. After dinner, I would like dessert.
c. After dinner, I would like wine .
d. After lunch, I would like dessert.

Translate to English

- Buenas noches. ¿Qué le puedo traer?

- Buenas, ¿Qué me recomienda?

- Este plato tiene carne, verduras, y pan y es muy delicioso.

- Está bien, me gustaría comer ese plato, entonces.

- ¿Y para beber?

- Me gustaría beber un vaso de vino, por favor.

- Está bien.

- Gracias, señor.

Chapter 8 Answers

Choose the correct answer

1. This dish has fish, vegetables, and bread.

a. Este plato tiene pescado, verduras, y pan

2. Can you bring me a beer please?

c. ¿Me puede traer una cerveza, por favor?

3. Excuse me ma'am, the check please.

d. Perdón señorita, la cuenta por favor.

4. Para el desayuno, hay pan, queso, y huevos.

c. For breakfast there is bread, cheese, and eggs.

5. Después de la cena, quisiera postre.

b. After dinner, I would like dessert.

Translate to English

- Buenas noches. ¿Qué le puedo traer?
- Buenas, ¿Qué me recomienda?
- Este plato tiene carne, verduras, y pan y es muy delicioso.
- Está bien, me gustaría comer ese plato, entonces.
- ¿Y para beber?
- Me gustaría beber un vaso de vino, por favor.
- Está bien.
- Gracias, señor.

- Good evening. What can I bring you?
- Good evening, what can you recommend?
- This dish has meat, vegetables, and bread and is very delicious.
- Okay, I would like that dish then.
- And to drink?

- I would like a glass of wine please.
- Okay.
- Thank you, sir.

Chapter 9
Going to the Doctor

¿Qué le pasa?

Let's talk about a not so fun but absolutely necessary event that you should be prepared for, going to the doctor or the hospital. Getting sick is no fun and even more difficult to deal with when you don't know how to communicate how you are feeling or what is wrong with you. It also can be a very likely event when you are in another country as you are eating food and are exposed to germs both of which your body is not used to. I remember living in Chile and becoming very ill after eating a traditional Chilean dish that is cooked in the ground and includes a mix of shellfish, meats, and sausages. I was taken to the hospital and would have definitely found the following phrases to be very useful. Below are some very basic and useful phrases to use when you are sick, going to the doctor, or hospital.

Phrases to use at the Doctor

What's wrong?	¿Qué le pasa?
I am sick.	Estoy enfermo/enferma.
I have a cold.	Estoy resfriado/a.
I have a headache.	Tengo dolor de la cabeza.
Sore throat	Dolor de garganta
You should rest.	Debe descansar.
Injection	La inyección
Cough	El tos
Fever	La fiebre
Medicine	Medicina
Prescription	La receta
Here is ...	Aquí está
Do you have health insurance?	¿Tiene seguro médico?

*Notice that there are two ways to say sick - (*enfermo* and *enferma*)

If you are a male = Estoy enferm**o**

If you are a female = Estoy enferm**a**

*The same goes for *resfriado* and *resfriada* along with many other adjectives

If you are a male = Estoy resfria**o**

If you are a female = Estoy resfria**a**

More Doctor Visit Vocabulary

Where does it hurt?	¿Dónde le duele?
It hurts here.	Me duele aquí.
My … hurts.	Me duele el/la …
Head	La cabeza
Arm	El brazo
Leg	La pierna
Stomach	El estómago
Hand	La mano
Foot	El pie
Eyes	Los ojos
Nose	La naríz
Mouth	La boca
Ear/Inner ear	La oreja/El oído
Chest	El pecho
I have diarrhea	Tengo diarrea
I have been vomiting	He estado vomitando

*When you want to talk about something that hurts

My leg hurts= Me duele la pierna.

His/her head hurts= Le duele la cabeza

Does your hand hurt =¿Te duele la mano?

* It is backwards and literally means- *the leg is hurting me, etc.*

¡La Práctica!

Fill in the blanks.

1. His arm hurts.

_____ duele el _____.

2. My foot hurts.

_____ duele el _____.

3. Does your head hurt?

¿_____ duele la _____?

4. Her chest hurts.

_____ duele el _____.

5. Where does it hurt?

¿_____ le _____?

Match the Vocabulary

1. arm ----------------------a. el estómago
2. chest----------------------b. la boca
3. foot ----------------------c. la cabeza
4. hand----------------------d. el pie
5. ear-------------------------e. el brazo
6. eyes----------------------f. la mano
7. leg-------------------------g. la oreja
8. mouth--------------------h. la pierna
9. stomach------------------i. los ojos
10. head---------------------j. el pecho

Translate to English

- Buenas tardes, ¿qué le pasa hoy?

- Estoy resfriada y tengo dolor de cabeza.

- ¿Tiene tos o dolor de garganta?

- Sí tengo tos y un poco de dolor de garganta.

- No tiene fiebre. Aquí está una receta.

- Gracias.

- ¿Tiene seguro médico?

- Sí, tengo.

- Está bien. Debe descansar mucho.

- Sí señor, muchas gracias.

- De nada, hasta luego.

Chapter 9 Answers

Fill in the blanks.

1. His arm hurts.

le duele el brazo .

2. My foot hurts.

Me duele el pie.

3. Does your head hurt?

¿ Te duele la cabeza?

4. Her chest hurts.

Le duele el pecho.

5. Where does it hurt?

¿Dònde le duele?

Match the Vocabulary

1. arm ----- e. el brazo

2. chest----- j. el pecho

3. Foot----- d. el pie

4. hand ----- f. la mano

5. ear--------g. la oreja

6. eyes----- i. los ojos

7. leg-------h. la pierna

8. mouth------ b. la boca

9. stomach----- a. el estómago

10. head----- c. la cabeza

Translate to English

- Buenas tardes, ¿qué le pasa hoy?
- Estoy resfriada y tengo dolor de cabeza.
- ¿Tiene tos o dolor de garganta?
- Sí tengo tos y un poco de dolor de garganta.
- No tiene flebre. Aquí está una receta.
- Gracias.
- ¿Tiene seguro médico?
- Sí, tengo.
- Está bien. Debe descansar mucho.
- Sí señor, muchas gracias.
- De nada, hasta luego.

- Good afternoon, what's wrong today?
- I have a cold and headache.
- Do you have a cough or sore throat?
- Yes I have a cough and a little bit of a sore throat.
- You don't have a fever. Here is a prescription.
- Thank you.
- Do you have health insurance?
- Yes, I do.
- Okay. You should get a lot of rest.
- Yes, sir. Thank you very much.
- Your welcome, see you later.

Chapter 10
Going to the Bank

Necesito retirar dinero

In this chapter we will discuss something that you definitely want to be well-informed on so that you don't make any major mistakes when dealing with your money. When you are traveling, studying, or working abroad you may choose to use a credit card, travelers cheques, an atm card, or to open your own bank account. In any of these cases, you will probably have to deal with going to the bank at least once during your stay, whether it be to transfer money home, withdraw, or exchange money. Below are some very useful phrases for you to deal with your money in a Spanish-speaking country.

Banking Phrases

I need to withdraw money	Necesito retirar dinero.
deposit money	depositar dinero
exchange money	cambiar dinero
How much is the dollar worth	¿A cómo está el dólar?
I want to open an account?	Quiero abrir una cuenta.
I want to transfer money.	Quiero transferir dinero.
Cash	En efectivo
Currency	Moneda

Vocabulario – En el banco

Credit Card	Tarjeta de crédito
Traveler's cheques	Cheques viajeros
Account	La cuenta
Cashier	Cajero
ATM	Cajero Automático
Loan	Préstamo
Identification (ID)	Identificación (ID)
Amount	Cantidad

¡La Práctica!

Match the Vocabulary

1. cajero ----------------------------------a. loan
2. cheques viajeros-----------------------b. credit card
3. la cuenta---------------------------------c. amount
4. el préstamo ---------------------------d. cashier
5. cajero automático---------------------e. currency
6. tarjeta de crédito---------------------f. ATM
7. cantidad-------------------------------g. cash
8. cambiar--------------------------------h. to exchange
9. moneda------------------------------- i. traveler's cheques
10. efectivo-------------------------------j. account

Translate to English

- ¿Buenas, cómo le puedo ayudar?

- Hola, necesito cambiar dinero.

- Está bien.

- ¿A cómo está el dólar?

- Un dólar está a trece pesos.

- Está bien, quiero cambiar cien dólares.

- Aquí está 1,300 pesos.

-Muchas gracias.

-De nada, gracias a Ud.

Chapter 10 Answers

Match the Vocabulary

1. cajero -------------------------d. cashier
2. cheques viajeros ------------i. traveler's cheques
3. la cuenta----------------------j. account
4. el préstamo ------------------a. loan
5. cajero automático-----------f. ATM
6. tarjeta de crédito------------b. credit card
7. cantidad----------------------c. amount
8. cambiar-----------------------h. to exchange
9. moneda-----------------------e. currency
10. efectivo---------------------g. cash

Translation

- ¿Buenas, cómo le puedo ayudar?
- Hola, necesito cambiar dinero.
- Está bien.
- ¿A cómo está el dólar?
- Un dólar está a trece pesos.
- Está bien, quiero cambiar cien dólares.
- Aquí está 1,300 pesos.
-Muchas gracias.
-De nada, gracias a Ud.

- Hello, how can I help you?
- Hi, I need to exchange money.
- Okay.
- How much is the dollar worth?
- The dollar is worth 13 pesos.
- Okay, I want to exchange 100 dollars.
- Here is 1,300 pesos.
-Thank you very much.
- Your welcome, thank you.

Chapter 11
Transportation

¿Adónde vamos?

Part 1: At the airport

This chapter will be divided into two sections: *At the Airport* and *Travelling by taxi, bus or train.* This section is dedicated to that ever exciting moment of arriving in the airport of the new country where you will study, play, sightsee, work or whatever your motive may be. It is true that most airport employees speak at least some English but in some cases, it will be very limited English so it is always helpful if you are one step ahead and know how to say a few useful things to get you through customs, outside of the airport, and ready to embark on your new adventure. Bon voyage or as they say in Spanish Buen viaje!

At the Airport

Airport	El Aeropuerto
Airplane	El Avión
Airline	La Aerolínea
Suitcase	La maleta
Passport	El pasaporte
Flight	El vuelo
Customs	La aduana
Ticket	El boleto
Baggage Claim Area	El reclamo de equipaje
Gate	La puerta
Terminal	La terminal
Destination	El destino
Have a good trip!	¡Buen viaje!

Useful Phrases at the Airport

When does the flight leave?	¿Cuándo sale el vuelo?
When does the flight arrive?	¿Cuándo llega el vuelo?
I have two suitcases.	Tengo dos maletas
Where is terminal B?	¿Dónde está la terminal B?

I´m looking for gate 17.	Busco la puerta 17.
Where is the baggage claim?	¿Dónde está el reclamo de equipaje?
My suitcases are lost.	Mis maletas están perdidas.

¡La Práctica!

Fill in the blank with the word from the word bank

El vuelo ----- maletas
La puerta -----   El boleto
La aerolínea ----- El reclamo de equipaje

1. Busco _____ veintitres.

2. ¿Cuando sale _____?

3. Mis maletas están en _____.

4. Voy a España con _____ de AirFrance.

5. Tengo muchas _____ que están en el reclamo de equipaje.

Match the Vocabulary

6. La aduana --------------------a. Airplane

7. El destino--------------------b. Customs

8. El boleto----------------------c. Have a good trip

9. El avión ----------------------d. Ticket

10. Buen viaje-------------------e. Destination

Translate to English

- Hola, señora ¿cómo le puedo ayudar?

- Hola, ¿cuándo sale el vuelo para Buenos Aires?

- Sale a las tres de la tarde..

- ¿De qué puerta sale?

- De la puerta diez.

- Está bien, muchas gracias señor.

- De nada, ¡buen viaje!

Part 2: Travelling by taxi, bus, or train.

This section is dedicated to that travelling you will do within the city or from city to city in your new country. Knowing how to read the signs and ask around inside of the various bus and train stations will hopefully help you avoid getting completely lost. And if you do, it will help you to get out of the situation. I always suggest being flexible and ready for adventure because sometimes getting lost just means you get to experience a completely new scenery you've never seen before. Within the city you may travel by bus, or taxi. Travelling by taxi is usually an excellent way to get language practice as you have your own personal conversation partner until you arrive to your destination. You will most likely travel by bus or train to go from city to city. Happy exploring in your new country!

Taxi Vocabulary

Where are we going?	¿Adónde vamos?
I'm going to…	Voy a …
At the stoplight, turn right/left	En el semáforo, dobla a la derecha/a la izquierda
You can stop here.	Puede parar aqui.
Here on the right/left	Aquí a la derecha/izquierda
How much do I owe you?	¿Cuánto le debo?

*As I mentioned in the intro, verbs in Spanish have more changes according to their subject. These are called **conjugations**.

* Below is the conjugation of the verb: *Ir- to go*

Ir- to go

Yo -------**Voy** ------- I go

tú-------- **Vas** -------you go

él, ella, Ud------- **Va**-------he, she goes; you (formal) go; it goes

nosotros, nosotras-------**Vamos** --------we go

ellos, ellas, Uds. ------- **Van** -------they, you all go

*Remember that you don't need to use the personal pronouns (I, he, she, et.) as often in Spanish.

Ex: I go = Voy (No need to say, *yo* **voy**)

you go = Vas (No need to say, *tú* **vas**)

* The personal pronoun is understood within the verb.

¡La Práctica!

Put the verb *ir* in the correct form.

1. Yo _____ a Chile mañana.

2. ¿Adónde _____ nosotros?

3. ¿Tú _____ al supermercado hoy?

4. ¿ Adónde _____ ella?

5. ¿Uds. _____ al restaurante?

Match the Phrases

6. En el semáforo dobla a la izquierda.----------------------a. Here on the right.

7. ¿Adónde vamos?----------------------b. How much do I owe you?

8. Aquí a la derecha---------------------c. You can stop here

9. Puede parar aquí---------------------d. Where are we going?

10. ¿Cuánto le debo? -------------------e. At the stoplight, turn left.

Bus and Train Vocabulary

The bus/train station	La estación de bus/tren
Bus stop	La parada de bus
When does the next train leave for…?	¿A qué hora sale el próximo tren para…?
Departures	Salidas
Llegadas	Arrivals
I would like a one way ticket	Quisiera un boleto de ida.
Round trip ticket	Boleto de ida y vuelta
Which platform does the train leave from?	¿De cuál andén sale el tren?
Do I need to change trains?	¿Necesito cambiar de tren?
To get on…	Subir
To get off..	Bajar

*Verb Conjugation

Salir- To leave

Yo-----------**Salgo** - -----------I leave
Tú -------------------------**Sales** ----------you leave
él, ella, Ud. ------------------**Sale** ----------**he, she leaves; you (formal) leave; it leaves**
nosotros, nosotras--------**Salimos** ------we leave
ellos, ellas, Uds. -----------**Salen** ---------**they, you all leave**

*Notice for *it leaves* you use the third conjugation, *sale.*

Ex: El tren **sale** a las 7 =The train **leaves** at 7

El bus **sale** a las 3:30 =The bus **leaves** at 3:30.

¡La Práctica!

Put the verb *salir* in the correct form.

11. Yo _____ para Caracas a las siete.

12. ¿A qué hora _____ el tren para Barcelona?

13. ¿Tú _____ a las seis para clase?

14. ¿ A qué hora _____ el bus para Santiago?

15. ¿A qué hora _____ ellos para San José?

Translate to English

- Buenos días, ¿Cómo le puedo ayudar?

- ¿A qué hora sale el próximo tren para Quito?

- Sale a las ocho de la mañana.

- Gracias. Quisiera un boleto de ida y vuelta para Quito.

- Está bien.
- ¿De cuál andén sale el tren?

- Sale del andén trece.

- Está bien, muchas gracias.

- De nada, buen viaje.

Fill in the blank with the word from the word bank

1. Busco la puerta veintitrés.

2. ¿Cuando sale el vuelo?

3. Mis maletas están en el reclamo de equipaje

4. Voy a España con la aerolínea de AirFrance.

5. Tengo muchas maletas que están en el reclamo de equipaje.

Match the Vocabulary

6. La aduana -------------b. Customs
7. El destino--------------e. Destination
9. El avión ---------------a. Airplane
10. Buen viaje------------c. Have a good trip.

Translation

- Hola, señora ¿cómo le puedo ayudar?
- Hola, ¿cuándo sale el vuelo para Buenos Aires?
- Sale a las tres de la tarde..
- ¿De qué puerta sale?
- De la puerta diez.
- Está bien, muchas gracias señor.
- De nada, ¡buen viaje!

- Hi, ma'am, how can I help you?
- Hi, when does the flight to Buenos Aires leave?
- It takes off at 3:00 pm.
- What gate does it leave from?
- From gate 10.
- Okay, thank you sir.
- Your welcome, bon voyage!

Chapter 11: Part 2 Answers

Put the verb *ir* in the correct form

1. Yo voy a Chile mañana.

2. ¿Adónde vamos nosotros?

3. ¿Tú vas al supermercado hoy?

4. ¿ Adónde va ella?

5. ¿Uds. van al restaurante?

Match the Phrases

6. En el semáforo dobla a la izquierda----- e. At the stoplight, turn left.

7. ¿Adónde vamos?----------------------------d. Where are we going?

8. Aquí a la derecha.---------------------------a. Here on the right

9. Puede parar aquí.----------------------------c. You can stop here.

10. ¿Cuánto le debo?---------------------------b. How much do I owe you?

Put the verb *salir* in the correct form

11. Yo salgo para Caracas a las siete.

12. ¿A qué hora sale el tren para Barcelona?

13. ¿Tú sales a las seis para clase?

14. ¿ A qué hora sale el bus para Santiago?

15. ¿A qué hora salen ellos para San José?

Translation

- Buenos días, ¿Cómo le puedo ayudar?

- ¿A qué hora sale el próximo tren para Quito?
- Sale a las ocho de la mañana.
- Gracias. Quisiera un boleto de ida y vuelta para Quito.
- Está bien.
- ¿De cuál andén sale el tren?
- Sale del andén trece.
- Está bien, muchas gracias.
- De nada, buen viaje.

- Good morning, how can I help you?
- What time does the next train leave for Quito?
- It leaves at 8 in the morning.
- Thank you. I would like a round trip ticket to Quito.
- Okay.
- Which platform does the train leave from?
- From platform 13.
- Okay, thank you very much.
- Your welcome, have a good trip.

Chapter 12
Finding a place to stay

Quisiera reservar una habitación

Now that we have hopefully gotten you to your destination safe and sound without having gotten lost too many times, it is time to look for a place to stay. Whether you decide to stay in a hotel, hostal, or bed and breakfast, this chapter should help you through every step of the way. Remember that some of the luxuries we are used to like *agua caliente* (hot water) cannot always be expected. Below, I have listed useful vocabulary and phrases for booking a room at your new destination. Enjoy your stay!

Hotel Vocabulary

I would like to reserve a room for one/two people.	Quisiera reservar una habitación para una/dos personas
How much does it cost per night?	¿Cuánto cuesta por la noche?
For how many people?	¿Para cuántas personas?
For how many nights?	¿Para cuántas noches?
Para una noche/dos noches	For one night/two nights
With a double bed.	Con una cama de matrimonio.
With two single beds	Con dos camas sencillas
I'm sorry, we are full.	Lo siento, está todo vendido
I have a reservation.	Tengo una reserva.
Do you have wi-fi?	¿Tiene wi-fi?

¡La Práctica!

Match the Phrases

1. I'm sorry we are full------------------------a. Tengo una reserva

2. For how many people?---------------------b. ¿Para cuántas noches?

3. I have a reservation.------------------------c. ¿Cuánto cuesta por la noche?

4. For how many nights?---------------------d. Lo siento, está todo vendido.

5. How much is it per night?------------------e. ¿Para cuántas personas?

Translate to English

- Buenas noches.

- Buenas noches, señorita, ¿cómo le puedo ayudar?

- Quisiera reservar una habitación para una persona.

- ¿Para cuántas noches

- Para tres noches.

- Está bien.

- ¿Cuánto cuesta por la noche?

- Cien dólares por noche.

- ¿Y aquí tiene wi-fi?

- Sí, tenemos wi-fi.

- Gracias, señor.

Match the Phrases

1. I'm sorry we are full----------------d. Lo siento, está todo vendido.
2. For how many people?-------------e. ¿Para cuántas personas?
3. I have a reservation.----------------a. Tengo una reserva.
4. For how many nights?--------------b. ¿Para cuántas noches?
5. How much is it per night?----------c. ¿Cuánto cuesta por la noche?

Translation

- Buenas noches.
- Buenas noches, señorita, ¿cómo le puedo ayudar?
- Quisiera reservar una habitación para una persona.
- ¿Para cuántas noches?
- Para tres noches.
- Está bien.
- ¿Cuánto cuesta por la noche?
- Cien dólares por noche.
- ¿Y aquí tiene wi-fi?
- Sí, tenemos wi-fi.
- Gracias, señor.

- Good evening.
- Good evening, ma'am, how can I help you?
- I would like to reserve a room for one person.
- For how many nights?
-- For three nights
- Okay.
- How much is it per night?
- 100 dollars per night.
- And do you have wi-fi?
- Yes, we have wi-fi.
- Thank you, sir.

SECTION 3
GETTING TO KNOW EACH OTHER

Chapter 13
Describing People & Things

¿Cómo es?

Now that we have gotten you through the essentials of getting around, finding a place to stay, and all of the other basics, we can focus on having a conversation in order to get to know people, make friends, etc. By the end of this section you will be able to talk about yourself, your family, work, and hobbies. The first chapter of this section is focused on description- how to describe yourself, other people, and things to others. Below, I have listed some useful vocabulary and phrases to help you describe the world around you.

Description Vocabulary

tall	alto/a
short	bajo/a
fat	gordo/a
thin	delgado/a
pretty	bonito/a
handsome	guapo/a
cute	lindo/a
hair	pelo
short (length)	corto/a
long	largo/a
big	grande
small	pequeño/a
strong	fuerte
ugly	feo/a
old	viejo/a
young	joven

*Why can most of the Spanish adjectives end in **o** or **a** like *lindo* or *linda*?

*Quick review- Which is correct, niño linda or niño lindo?

*If you said niñ**o** lind**o**, you are right!
Don't forget to match the adjective to gender of the noun.

Description Phrases and More Vocabulary

What's it like?	¿Cómo es?
What does he/she look like?	¿Cómo es él/ella?
He is…/She is …	Él es …/Ella es …
I am…	Soy …
What color is his/her hair?	¿De qué color es su pelo?
His/her hair is….	Su pelo es ….
Does she have long hair?	¿Ella tiene el pelo largo?
He has short hair.	Él tiene el pelo corto.
blonde	rubio/a
brunette	castaño
red headed	pelirrojo/a

*Verb Conjugation

Ser- to be (permanent)

Yo-------------Soy------------I am

Tú------------Eres-----------you are

él, ella, Ud.----Es-------------he, she is; you (formal) are; it is

nosotros, nosotras-----Somos----we are

ellos, ellas, Uds.-----Son-------they, you all are

¡La práctica!

Put the verb *ser* in the correct form and translate the sentence.

1. Yo_____ muy alta y delgada--
_____

2. Ella _____ es baja y linda.------
_____

3. ¿Él _____ muy viejo?-----------
_____

4. Nosotros _____ guapos.--------
_____

5. Ellos _____ fuertes. --------------
_____

Translate the Phrases

1. ¿Cómo es ella? --------------------------
_____

2. Ella es alta, joven, y bonita.------------
_____

3. ¿De qué color es su pelo?--------------
_____

4. Ella tiene el pelo rubio y largo.--------
_____

5. ¿Él tiene el pelo corto?------------------
_____

6. Sí, tiene el pelo corto y negro.---------
_____

*Below I will list some words to describe your emotions. You should use forms of the verb *estar* to talk about your emotions.

Ex: estoy contenta.=I am happy.

Emotion Vocabulary

How do you feel?	¿Cómo te sientes?
I feel…	Me siento…
Happy	Felíz, Contento/a
Sad	Triste
Tired	Cansado/a
Excited	Emocionado/a
Bored	Aburrido/a
Angry	Enojado/a
Nervous	Nervioso/a
Calm	Tranquilo/a
Busy	Ocupado/a
Scared	Asustado/a

*Verb Conjugation

Estar- to be (Temporary)

Yo----**Estoy**-----**I am**

Tú------**Estás**-------**you are**

él, ella, Ud------**Está**-------**he, she is; you (formal) are; it is**

nosotros, nosotras-----**Estamos**-----**we are**

ellos, ellas, Uds.------ **Están**------**they, you all are**

Match the Vocabulary

1. happy--a. aburrido
2. excited--b. ocupada
3. nervous---c. cansada
4. bored--d. asustado
5. angry--e. enojado
6. sad --f. tranquila
7. calm--g. felíz
8. busy--h. emocionado
9. scared---i. triste
10. tired---j. nerviosa

Put the verb *estar* in the correct form and translate the sentence.

1. Yo _____ muy triste._____

2. Ella _____ contenta hoy._____

3. ¿Él _____ nervioso?_____

4. Nosotros _____ tranquilos._____

5. Ellas _____ asustados.
_____

Put the verb *ser* in the correct form and translate the sentence.

1. Yo soy muy alta y delgada. ------ I am very tall and thin.

2. Ella es baja y linda. -------------- She is short and cute.

3. ¿Él es muy viejo?----------------- Is he very old?

4. Nosotros somos guapos. ------- We are very handsome.

5. Ellos son fuertes. ------------------ They are strong.

Translate the Phrases

1. ¿Cómo es ella? ---------------------------- What is she like?

2. Ella es alta, joven, y bonita.------------- She is tall, young, and pretty.

3. ¿De qué color es su pelo?---------------- What color is his/her hair?

4. Ella tiene el pelo rubio y largo.-------- She has long and blonde hair.

5. ¿Él tiene el pelo corto? ------------------ Does he have short hair?

6. Sí, tiene el pelo corto y negro---------- Yes, he has short, black hair.

Match the Vocabulary

1. happy ------------g. felíz
2. Excited-----------h. emocionado
3. Nervous---------j. nerviosa
4. bored -----------a. aburrido
5. Angry-------------e. enojado
6. Sad----------------i. triste
7. Calm--------------f. tranquila
8. Busy-------------b. ocupada
9. Scared-----------d. asustado

10. Tired----------c. cansada

Put the verb *estar* in the correct form and translate the sentence.

1. Yo estoy muy triste.----------------I am very sad.
2. Ella está contenta hoy. -----------She is happy today.
3. ¿Él está nervioso?------------------Is he nervous?
4. Nosotros estamos tranquilos.-----We are calm.
5. Ellas están asustados.--------------They are scared.

Chapter 14
We are Family!

¿Cuántos hermanos tiene?

In this chapter you will be able to talk about your family – how many brothers and sisters you have, are they older or younger, etc. You will also be able to talk about your more extended family- aunts, uncles, cousins, grandparents, etc. When you travel to a Spanish-speaking country, you will realize the importance that family plays in an individual's life. Families are very close and place emphasis on taking care of one another. We will also learn the conjugation of a very useful verb *tener* so you can discuss what you and others have. Below you will learn useful language to describe your family.

Family vocabulary and phrases

How many siblings do you have?	¿Cuántos hermanos tiene?
I have 3 siblings.	Tengo 3 hermanos.
Brother	hermano
Sister	hermana
Mom	mamá
Dad	papá
Mother	madre
Father	padre
grandpa/grandma	abuelo/abuela
cousin (female/male)	primo/prima
husband/wife	esposo/esposa
son/daughter	hijo/hija
uncle/aunt	tío/tía
Pet	mascota
Dog	perro
Cat	gato
Older	mayor
Younger	menor

* Remember that the adjective comes after noun.
younger brother = hermano menor
older sister = hermana mayor

*Verb Conjugation

Tener- to have
Yo --------------------Tengo -------------I have
Tú---------------------Tienes-------------you have
él, ella, Ud.-------------Tiene -------------he, she has; you (formal) have; it has
nosotros, nosotras---**Tenemos** --------we have
ellos, ellas, Uds.-------**Tienen**------------they, you all have

*It's useful to know the possessive pronouns in order to talk about family, so you can say – *my* mom, *his* sister, *her* grandma, etc.

Possessive Pronouns

My	Mi/Mis
Your	Tu/Tus
His or Her	Su/Sus
Our	Nuestro/Nuestra/Nuestros/Nuestras
Their	Su/Sus

*Notice you have to match it with the number of what is yours and for *nuestro* the number and the gender.
Ex: My brother = Mi hermano
My siblings = Mis hermanos
Our grandma = Nuestra abuela

¡La Práctica!

Put the verb *tener* in the correct form and translate the sentence.

1. Yo_____tres hermanos.
_____

2. Él _____ diez primos.
_____

3. ¿Ella _____ muchos hermanos?
_____

4. Nosotros _____ dos hijos.
_____

5. Ellos _____ un perro y un gato.
_____

Match the Vocabulary

1. esposo---a. grandma

2. esposa---b. pet

3. tío---c. older

4. tía ---d. aunt

5. mayor---e. dad

6. menor---f. grandpa

7. mascota---g. husband

8. abuelo--h. wife

9. abuela--i. younger

10. papá---j. uncle

Put the possessive pronoun in the correct form

1. (My) _____ hermanos son muy altos.

2. (His) _____ hermana es bonita.

3. (Our) _____ abuela es muy simpática.

4. ¿(Your) _____ padres son bajos?

5. (Their) _____ abuelos son muy viejos?

Write about your family following the example

Yo tengo un hermano mayor. Él tiene 33 años y se llama Jacob. Él tiene una esposa que se llama Annie. Mi mamá se llama Ruth y mi papá se llama Keith. Tengo doce primos en total. Son tres primos y nueve primas. También tengo un esposo y un hijo. Se llaman Alberto y Elijah. Tengo dos abuelos que viven en Texas y una abuela que vive en Oklahoma.

Chapter 14 Answers

Put the verb *tener* in the correct form and translate the sentence.

1. Yo <u>tengo</u> tres hermanos. ---------------<u>I have three brothers.</u>
2. Él <u>tiene</u> diez primos. ------------------<u>He has ten cousins.</u>
3. ¿Ella <u>tiene</u> muchos hermanos?------<u>Does she have many siblings?</u>
4. Nosotros <u>tenemos</u> dos hijos.---------<u>We have two children.</u>
5. Ellos <u>tienen</u> un perro y un gato. -------<u>They have a dog and a cat.</u>

Match the Vocabulary

1. esposo ---------g. husband
2. esposa ----------h. wife
3. tío --------------j. uncle
4. tío --------------d. aunt
5. mayor----------c. older
6. menor----------i. younger
7. mascota-------b. husband
8. abuelo---------f. grandpa
9. abuela----------a. grandma
10. papá ----------e. dad

Put the possessive pronoun in the correct form

1. (My) <u>Mis</u> hermanos son muy altos.

2. (HIs) <u>Su</u> hermana es bonita.

3. (Our) <u>Nuestra</u> abuela es muy simpática.

4. ¿ (Your) <u>Tus or Sus</u> padres son bajos?

5. (Their) <u>Sus</u> abuelos son muy viejos?

Write about your family following the example

Various possible answers.

Chapter 15
All Work and No Play?

¿En qué trabaja Ud.?

Now that we are able to describe ourselves physically and discuss our family, we can talk about what we do, our career. It is something that we often talk about and sometimes unfortunately can consume our lives. In Latin American culture, they are often surprised at how work is such a big part of our lives. As I mentioned in the previous chapter, helping each other out as friends and family is often more important than one's individual career and success. In this chapter, you will learn some basic professions of our society.

Occupational vocabulary and phrases

What do you do?	¿En qué trabaja Ud.?
I am a teacher.	Soy profesora.
teacher	profesor/profesora
businessman/business woman	empresario/empresaria
Doctor	medico/médica
Nurse	enfermero/enfermera
Lawyer	abogado/abogada
Writer	escritor/escritora
policeman	policia
firefighter	bombero/bombera
student	estudiante
receptionist	recepcionista
Waiter	mesero/mesera
Cook	cocinero/cocinera
salesperson	vendedor/vendedora
engineer	ingeniero/ingeniera

*By now, you can probably guess why most of the occupations end in either *o* or *a*

Ex: abogadp = lawyer (male)

Abogada = lawyer (female)

*Spanish differentiates between females and males much more often in its words. You notice when you say lawyer in English, we don't know whether the person is a he or she, in Spanish, you immediately know.

¡La Práctica!

Match the Vocabulary

1. abogada-----------------------------------a. police officer

2. bombero-----------------------------------b. nurse

3. mesero-------------------------------------c. doctor

4. cocinera ----------------------------------d. businessman

5. ingienera----------------------------------e. salesperson

6. enfermero---------------------------------f. waiter

7. empresario--------------------------------g. firefighter

8. vendedor----------------------------------h. attorney

9. médica-------------------------------------i. engineer

10. policía------------------------------------j. cook

Put the correct form of the word according to gender.

1. Ella es una _____ (abogado/abogada).

2. Ellos son _____ (bomberos/bombero).

3. Él es un _____ (profesor/profesora).

4. Ellas son _____ (escritores/escritoras).

5. Soy _____ (un empresario/una empresaria). (Answer according to your gender)

Answer the following question about your occupation. Don't forget to answer according to your gender.

¿En qué trabaja Ud.?
_____
_____

Match the Vocabulary

1. abogada ------h. attorney
2. bombero------g. firefighter
3. mesero--------f. waiter
4. cocinera ------j. cook
5. ingienera-----i. engineer
6. enfermero----b. nurse
7. empresario----d. businessman
8. vendedor-----e. salesperson
9. médica ------c. doctor
10. policía------a. police officer

Put the correct form of the word according to gender.

1. Ella es una abogada (abogado/abogada).

2. Ellos son bomberos (bomberos/bombero).

3. Él es un profesor (profesor/profesora).

4. Ellas son escritoras (escritores/escritoras).

5. Soy answers will vary (un empresario/una empresaria). (Answer according to your gender)

¿En qué trabaja Ud.?

Answers will vary.

Chapter 16
Hobbies

¿Qué le gusta hacer?

Now that we have learned how to describe yourself, your family, and occupation, we can move onto discussing what you enjoy doing in your free time. Once again, a cultural difference that you will see in Latin American countries is that they often spend their free time with family in contrast to our culture in which we more often look for our own individual hobbies and interests and try to spend most of our free time with our friends, away from family. Below you will find useful phrases to discuss our hobbies and also an explanation of the verb *gustar* so that you can talk about what you like.

Vocabulary to discuss your Hobbies

What do you like to do? (formal)	¿Qué **le** gusta hacer?
What do you like to do? (informal)	¿Qué **te** gusta hacer?
I like ...	Me gusta...
I don't like	No me gusta...
free time	tiempo libre
play sports	jugar deportes
play videogames	jugar videojuegos
travel	viajar
read	leer
go to the movies	ir al cine
go to the beach	ir a la playa
watch TV	ver televisión
watch sports	ver deportes
listen to music	escuchar música
play an instrument	tocar un instrumento
ski	esquiar
spend time with friends	pasar tiempo con amigos

*Notice that most of the verbs in Spanish end in *ar, er, ir*. These are called infinitives.

Ex: jugar = to play

*You will learn how to conjugate regular verbs in the last section of this book.

* The verb *gustar- to like* is conjugated very differently than other verbs. This is because when you say, *I like* in Spanish, you are literally saying *it is pleasing to me*. Below, I will outline the ways to use *gustar* with different people doing the liking.

A mí -----**me gusta**-----I like…

A ti-------**te gusta**…------You like…

A él-------**le gusta**…------He likes…

A ella-----**le gusta**…------She likes…

A nosotros/---**nos gusta**…---We like
nosotras

A ellos/-----**les gusta**…------They like…
ellas

A Uds.-----**les gusta**…------You all like…

*You do not have to use the first two words (*A mí*) of these phrases you can simply say *me gusta.*

Ex: You like to ski = Te gusta esquiar

We like to travel – Nos gusta viajar

* The only time you need to use the first two words is if it is unclear who is doing the liking because with *le* and *les gusta*, you are not always sure…

Ex: They like =A ellos les gusta

She likes =A ella le gusta

* If you want to say, *I don't like* simply add *no* in front of the *me, te, le, or les*.

Ex: You don't like = No te gusta

He doesn't like   =   (A él) no le gusta

¡La Práctica!

Choose the correct answer

1. I like to go to the movies.

a. Le gusta ir al a playa.---------------b. Te gusta ir al cine.

c. Me gusta ir al cine. .----------------d. Me gusta ir a la playa.

2. Do you like to read?

a. ¿Te gusta tocar? --------------------b. ¿Les gusta leer?

c. ¿Nos gusta tocar? .--------------------d. ¿Te gusta leer?

3. I don't like to travel.
a. Me no gusta viajar-------------- b. Me no gusta jugar.
c. No le gusta jugar------------------d. No me gusta viajar.

Match the Verb Phrases
1. Jugar deportes----------------------------------a. Spend time with friends
2. Ir a la playa --------------------------------------b. Play videogames
3. Pasar tiempo con amigos   ------------------ c. Watch sports.
4. Ver deportes ------------------------------------ d. Go to the beach
5. Jugar videojuegos------------------------------e. Play sports

Choose the correct answer

1. I like to go to the movies.

c. Me gusta ir al cine.

2. Do you like to read?

d. ¿Te gusta leer?

3. I don't like to travel.

d. No me gusta viajar.

Match the Verb Phrases

1. Jugar deportes   e. Play sports
2. Ir a la playa   d. Go to the beach
3. Pasar tiempo con amigos   a. Spend time with friends
4. Ver deportes   c. Watch sports.
5. Jugar videojuegos   b. Play videogames

SECTION 4
GRAMMAR SCHOOL

Chapter 17
To Be or Not to Be... That's the Question!

Ser y Estar

In the last section of this crash course we will discuss some of the difficult grammar topics of Spanish in the simplest way possible. As I have said, languages cannot be translated word for word and often one word in one language can be communicated in more than one way depending on the situation. One of these words in English is *to be* which in Spanish can be said in two ways *ser* or *estar* depending on the specific circumstances. We find this difficult because we must think harder about what is being or not being. Below I will explain when to use each and we will review how to conjugate these verbs.

Ser- to be (Generally for permanent states)

Rule	English Example	Spanish Example
Origin	I am from Spain.	Soy de España.
Description	Her car is red.	Su carro es rojo.
Occupation	I am a nurse.	Soy enfermera.
Date	Today is January 4th.	Hoy es el 4 de enero.
Time	It is 3:00.	Son las 3:00.
Characteristic	She is tall.	Ella es alta

Estar-to be (Generally used for temporary conditions)

Rule	English Example	Spanish Example
Position	My house is next to the post office.	Mi casa está al lado del correo.
Action	He is travelling to Chile.	Él está viajando a Chile.
Condition	Are you sick?	¿Estás enferma?
Emotion	I'm bored.	Estoy aburrido.

*Let's look at some differences between *ser* and *estar*

Ser is used to talk about the general characteristic of something.

Estar is used to talk about the condition of something.
Ex: Bananas are yellow. = Los plátanos son amarillos. *(In general bananas are yellow)*
This banana is green. = Este plátano está verde *(This specific banana is green now and it could change)*

Pescado es delicioso.= Fish is delicious *(Generally speaking, fish is delicious)*
Este pescado está delicioso = This fish is delicious.
(This fish I am eating now is delicious)
*Do you get the general idea now?
- *ser* describes the general charactistic of things.
- *estar* describes the specific state of things in this moment.

¡La Práctica!

See if you can remember how to conjugate the verbs *Ser* and *Estar* below

Ser- to be (permanent)
Yo _____
Tú _____
él, ella, Ud. _____
nosotros, nosotras _____
ellos, ellas, Uds_____

Estar- to be (temporary)
yo_____
tú_____
él, ella, Ud._____
nosotros, nosotras_____
ellos, ellas, Uds. _____

Fill in the blank with the correct form of *ser* or *estar*
1. Yo _____ (soy/estoy) de Estados Unidos.
2. El perro _____ (es/está) negro.
3. Él _____ (es/está) muy contento.
4. Ellas _____ (son/están) profesores.
5. El correo _____ (es/está) al lado del supermercado.

6. Nosotros _____ (somos/estamos) hablando español.
7. Yo _____ (soy/estoy) muy alta.
8. _____ (son/están) las cinco de la tarde.
9. ¿Tú _____ (eres/estás) enfermo?
10. Hoy _____ (es/está) el cinco de mayo.

See if you can remember how to conjugate the verbs *Ser* and *Estar* below

Ser- to be (permanent)

Yo ------ Soy
Tú------ Eres
él, ella, Ud.-------- Es
nosotros, nosotras ------ Somos
ellos, ellas, Uds.--------- Son

Estar- to be (temporary)

Yo ------- Estoy
Tú ------ Estás
él, ella, Ud ------Está
nosotros, nosotras -----Estamos
ellos, ellas, Uds. -----Estàn

Fill in the blank with the correct form of *ser* or *estar*

1. Yo soy (soy/estoy) de Estados Unidos.

2. El perro es (es/está) negro.

3. Él está (es/está) muy contento.

4. Ellas son (son/están) profesores.

5. El correo está (es/está) al lado del supermercado.

6. Nosotros estamos (somos/estamos) hablando español.

7. Yo   soy (soy/estoy) muy alta.

8. Son (son/están) las cinco de la tarde.

9. ¿Tú estás (eres/estás) enfermo?

10. Hoy es (es/está) el cinco de mayo.

Chapter 18
"Por" y "Para"

In this chapter we will discuss the differences between *por* and *para*. They can both be translated as *for* and for this reason can be quite confusing to non-native speakers of Spanish. I will clear up this confusion and explain when to use each below.

Por- Generally used to express movement through time or space

Rule	English Example	Spanish Example
To show thanks	Thank you for your help	Gracias por su ayuda.
Per (time period)	How much is it per night?	Cuánto es por la noche?
To show length of time	I studied for 5 hours.	Estudié por 5 horas.
To show means of transportation	I am going by train.	Voy por tren.
To show means of communication	We talk on Skype.	Hablamos por Skype.
To show what time of day	I go in the morning.	Voy por la mañana
To show the reason for something	I am sick because of the weather	Estoy enferma por el clima.
In exchange for something	I paid $5 for the sandwich.	Pagué $5 por el sandwich.
Going through a place/area	I am going through the park.	Voy por el parque

Para – Generally used to show destination for something.

Rule	English Example	Spanish Example
Showing your destination (place)	The train leaves for Caracas at 3.	El tren sale para Caracas a las 3.
Showing for whom something is	The surprise is for Lorena.	La sorpresa es para Lorena.
Showing when something is due	The homework is due Monday.	La tarea es para el lunes.
To show a goal for	I study a lot in order to	Estudio mucho para ser

| something | be smart. | inteligente. |

Other common and useful phrases with por and para

- por ejemplo ----- for example
- por ciento -------- percent
- por eso ---------- that's why
- por fin ------------- finally
- por favor ----------please
- por aquí ----------around here

- para que -------- so that
- ¿Para qué? --------why? for what purpose?
- para entonces --------by that time
- para siempre-----------forever

¡La Práctica!

Put *por* or *para* in the blank.

1. Voy a clase _____ la mañana.

2. Tengo una sorpresa _____ mi mamá.

3. El bus sale _____ San Juan a las dos.

4. Hablamos _____ teléfono.

5. ¿Uds. van _____ tren a la capital?

6. La tarea es _____ el miércoles.

7. ¿_____ qué no vas por avión?

8. La cuenta _____ favor.

9. Muchas gracias _____ el regalo.

10. Estudio mucho _____ ir a la universidad.

Put *por* or *para* in the blank.

1. Voy a clase por la mañana.

2. Tengo una sorpresa para mi mamá.

3. El bus sale para San Juan a las dos.

4. Hablamos por teléfono.

5. ¿Uds. van por tren a la capital?

6. La tarea es para el miércoles.

7. ¿Por qué no vas por avión?

8. La cuenta por favor.

9. Muchas gracias por el regalo.

10. Estudio mucho para ir a la universidad.

Chapter 19
Conjugating Regular Verbs in the Present

Another confusing aspect of Spanish is the need for so many verb changes. In English, we usually have two changes in the present. For example, *I walk,* you *walk,* he or she *walks,* we *walk,* etc. It only changes in the *he* or *she* form from *walk* to *walks*. In Spanish, you would have five changes for this verb. Regular verbs are divided into three kinds: verbs that end in *ar, er,* or *ir* verbs. We have already conjugated throughout this book several irregular and commonly used verbs. Below, we will discuss conjugating mostly regular verbs in the present and a few more common irregular verbs.

Steps for Conjugating Regular Present Verbs:

1. Remove the ending: *ar, er,* or *ir*

2. Identify what the subject is: *I, you, he, she, we,* etc.

3. Attach the corresponding ending to the verb.

'ar' verbs

Habl*ar*- to talk > remove the *ar* > *habl* > attach the correct ending

yo	**o**	habl**o**	=	I talk
tú	**as**	habl**as**	=	you talk
él, ella, Ud.	**a**	habl**a**	=	he, she talks; you talk
nosotros, nosotras	**amos**	habl**amos**	=	we talk
ellos, ellas, Uds.	**an**	habl**an**	=	they, you all talk

*Let's say you want to say *we walk:*

Caminar- to walk > remove the *ar* > camin >

attach the correct ending- *amos* = caminamos- we walk

'er' verbs

Comer- to eat > remove the *er* > com > attach the correct ending

yo	**o**	com**o**	=	I eat
tú	**es**	com**es**	=	you eat
él, ella, Ud.	**e**	com**e**	=	he, she eats; you eat
nosotros, nosotras	**emos**	com**emos**	=	we eat
ellos, ellas, Uds.	**en**	com**en**	=	they, you all eat

*Note- *ir* verbs have the same ending as *er* except in the *nosotros* it changes to *imos*

'ir' verbs

Vivir- to live> remove the *ir* > viv > attach the correct ending

yo	**o**	viv**o**	=	I live
tú	**es**	viv**es**	=	you live
él, ella, Ud.	**e**	viv**e**	=	he, she lives; you live
nosotros, nosotras	**imos**	viv**imos**	=	we live
ellos, ellas, Uds.	**en**	viv**en**	=	they, you all live

¡La Práctica!

Put the verbs in the correct form and translate the sentences.

1. Él _____ (viajar) a Chile mañana.
_____

2. Yo _____ (comer) mucha ensalada.
_____

3. ¿Tú _____ (leer) mucho?
_____

4. ¿Ella _____ (vivir) en Nueva York?
_____

5. ¿Uds. _____ (hablar) español?
_____

6. Nosotros _____ (esquiar) en los Andes.
_____

7. ¿Ud. _____ (escuchar) música rock?
_____

8. Ellos _____ (tocar) un instrumento.
_____

9. Yo _____ (pasar) tiempo con amigos.
_____

10. ¿Uds. _____ (vivir) en Tegucigalpa?
_____

Common Irregular Verb Conjugations

Throughout the previous chapters we have already conjugated the following common irregular verbs: *estar, ser, tener, gustar,* and *ir*. In this chapter we will add five more of the most used verbs in the Spanish language: *poder, querer, saber, decir,* and *hacer*.

poder- to be able to
querer- to want
saber- to know
decir- to say
hacer- to do/make

Poder- to be able to

yo	**Puedo -**	I can
tú	**Puedes -**	you can

él, ella, Ud.	**Puede** -	he, she can; you (formal) can
nosotros, nosotras	**Podemos** -	we can
ellos, ellas, Uds.	**Pueden** -	they, you all can

*In order to say: I can do something, just add the *infinitive* after the form of *poder*.

    Ex: I can ski   =   Puedo esquiar
    We can go today.   =   Podemos ir hoy.

Querer- to want

yo	**Quiero** -	I want
tú	**Quieres** -	you want
él, ella, Ud.	**Quiere** -	he, she wants; you (formal) can
nosotros, nosotras	**Queremos** -	we want
ellos, ellas, Uds.	**Quieren** -	they, you all want

Saber- to know

yo	**Sé-**	I know
tú	**Sabes** -	you know
él, ella, Ud.	**Sabe** -	he, she knows; you (formal) know
nosotros, nosotras	**Sabemos** -	we know
ellos, ellas, Uds.	**Saben** -	they, you all know

Hacer- to do/to make

yo	**Hago** -	I do/make
tú	**Haces** -	you do/make
él, ella, Ud.	**Hace** -	he, she does/makes; you (formal) do/make
nosotros, nosotras	**Hacemos** -	we do/make
ellos, ellas, Uds.	**Hacen** -	they, you do/make

Decir- to say

yo	**Digo** -	I say

tú	**Dices** - you say	
él, ella, Ud.	**Dice** -	he, she says; you (formal) say
nosotros, nosotras	**Decimos** -	we say
ellos, ellas, Uds.	**Dicen** - they, you say	

* I am going to also conjugate *decir* in the past tense because of how frequently it is used. Decir in the past can mean- said, told, spoke

Decir- to say (Past tense)

yo   **Dije** -   I said/told

tú   **Dijiste** -   you said/told

él, ella, Ud.   **Dijo** -   he, she said/told; you (formal) said/told

nosotros, nosotras   **Dijimos** -   we said/told

ellos, ellas, Uds.   **Dijeron** -   they, you said/told

*Useful phrases with *decir*- Some of the most frequently said things that I found very useful when I first lived in a Spanish-speaking country.

(él/ella) **me dijo**	=	(he/she) **told me**
le dije	=	**I told** him/her/you
te dije	=	**I told you**
les dije	=	**I told** them/you all

¡La Práctica!

Put the verbs in the correct form.

1. Ella _____ (poder) hablar inglés.
2. Yo _____ (saber) esquiar muy bien.
3. ¿Tú _____ (querer) ir a la playa?
4. Ellas _____ (hacer) la tarea de matemáticas.
5. ¿Ud. _____ (saber) hablar español?

Put the verbs in the correct form and translate the sentences.

6. Nosotros _____ (poder) ir al cine.
_____

7. ¿Qué _____ (hacer) Uds. en su tiempo libre? _____

8. Ellos _____ (querer) ir a Argentina.
_____

9. Yo _____ (decir- past) hola.
_____

10. ¿Uds. _____ (poder) ver televisión?
_____

Translate into Spanish.

11. I told him _____
12. He told me _____
13. I told you _____
14. I told them _____
15. She told me _____

Chapter 19 Answers

Put the verbs in the correct form and translate the sentences.

1. Él <u>viaja</u> (viajar) a Chile mañana.   He travels to Chile tomorrow.
2. Yo <u>como</u> (comer) mucha ensalada.   I eat a lot of salad.
3. ¿Tú <u>lees</u> (leer) mucho?   Do you read a lot?
4. ¿Ella <u>vive</u> (vivir) en Nueva York?   Does she live in New York?
5. ¿Uds. <u>hablan</u> (hablar) español?   Do you all speak Spanish?
6. Nosotros <u>esquiamos</u> (esquiar) en los Andes.   We ski in the Andes.
7. ¿Ud. <u>escuchan</u> (escuchar) música rock?   Do you listen to rock music?
8. Ellos <u>tocan</u> (tocar) un instrumento.   They play an instrument.
9. Yo <u>paso</u> (pasar) tiempo con amigos.   I spend time with friends.
10. ¿Uds. <u>viven</u> (vivir) en Tegucigalpa?   Do you all live in Tegucigalpa?

Put the verbs in the correct form.

1. Ella <u>puede</u> (poder) hablar inglés.
2. Yo <u>sé</u> (saber) esquiar muy bien.
3. ¿Tú <u>quieres</u> (querer) ir a la playa?
4. Ellas <u>hacen</u> (hacer) la tarea de matemáticas.
5. ¿Ud. <u>saben</u> (saber) hablar español?

Put the verbs in the correct form and translate the sentences.

6. Nosotros <u>podemos</u> (poder) ir al cine.   We can go to the movies.
7. ¿Qué <u>hacen</u> (hacer) Uds. en su tiempo libre?   What do you all do in your free time?
8. Ellos <u>quieren</u> (querer) ir a Argentina.   They want to go to Argentina.
9. Yo <u>dije</u> (decir- past) hola.   I said hi.
10. ¿Uds. <u>pueden</u> (poder) ver televisión?   Can you all watch tv?

Translate into Spanish.

11. I told him   <u>Le dije</u>
12. He told me   <u>Èl me dijo</u>
13. I told you   <u>Te dije</u>
14. I told them   <u>Les dije</u>
15. She told me   <u>Ella me dijo</u>

Chapter 20
Tener o No Tener

To have hunger, to have sleepiness, to have thirst???

In this last chapter we will deal with the unusual way in which you express certain feelings or needs that you have. In English, we often use the verb- *to be. I am hot, you are cold, he is scared*, etc. Instead of saying, *I am hungry, I am thirsty, I am sleepy*; you say that *you have* all of these feelings or conditions. This is not used with every adjective that expresses how you feel, so you must memorize in which situations *tener* should be used. Some of the situations in which you should use *tener* include when you are describing being sleepy, hungry, thirsty, scared, hot, cold, and even including when you are telling your age. *I have* thirty years, instead of *I am* thirty years old. It's a strange thing for us English speakers to comprehend but as I have said many times, NO language can be translated word for word. We have to remember to instead translate the ideas and keep in mind that in each language ideas are expressed in very different ways. Below, I have listed some 'tener expressions' with some questions for practice.

List of 'tener expressions'

tener _____ años-   to be ___ years old

tener hambre -   to be hungry

tener sed -   to be thirsty

tener frío -   to be cold

tener calor -   to be hot

tener sueño -   to be sleepy

tener prisa -   to be in a hurry

tener miedo -   to be scared

tener cuidado -	to be careful
¡ten cuidado!	Be careful!
tener razón -	to be right
tener éxito -	to be successful
tener celos -	to be jealous
tener suerte -	to be lucky
tener la culpa -	to be guilty
tener ganas de-	to feel like (doing something)
tener confianza -	to be confident
tener verguenza -	to be embarrassed

Note: If you want to emphasize the feeling, I am very thirsty, sleepy, etc., in most cases you add 'mucho' or 'mucha' before the adjective.
Ex: tengo **mucha** hambre = I am **very** hungry
Tienes **mucho** sueño   = You are **very** sleepy
Tenemos **mucho** sed   = We are **very** thirsty

¡La Práctica!

Translate the expressions into English

1. Hoy tengo mucho sueño._____

2. ¿Cuántos años tienes?_____

3. Tengo treinta años.
_____

4. Tenemos mucho frío.
_____

5. ¿Tienes sed? ¿Quieres tomar agua?_____

6. Tengo mucho calor. Sí, quiero tomar agua._____

7. ¡Tengo mucho miedo de los cocodrilos!
_____

8. ¡Ten cuidado! Hay un perro muy grande.
_____

9. Mi amigo tiene mucha suerte. ¡Ganó 1,000 dólares!
_____

10. Tengo ganas de comer pizza.
_____

Tip: Remember to use context clues if you don't know a word. Making an educated guess based on the words is always helpful! It's one of the most important skills to have when learning a language.

Translate the expressions into English

1. Hoy tengo mucho sueño.-------------I am very sleepy today.

2. ¿Cuántos años tienes?   ----------------How old are you?

3. Tengo treinta años. -------------------I am thirty years old.

4. Tenemos mucho frío. -------------------We are very cold.

5. ¿Tienes sed? ¿Quieres tomar agua?---------------Are you thirsty? Do you want to drink water?

6. Tengo mucho calor. Sí, quiero tomar agua.----------------I am very hot. Yes, I want to drink water.

7. ¡Tengo mucho miedo de los cocodrilos! ------------I am very scared of crocodiles.

8. ¡Ten cuidado! Hay un perro muy grande. -------------Be careful! There is a very big dog.

9. Mi amigo tiene mucha suerte. ¡Ganó 1,000 dólares!-------------My friend is very lucky. He won 1,000 dollars.

10. Tengo ganas de comer pizza. -------I feel like eating pizza.

Conclusion

Aren't You Excited? Your Journey Is About to Begin!

Now you are ready to go out there and start communicating in the basic Spanish that you have learned from this book. Keep in mind that you have not learned how to say *everything* in Spanish, but you are equipped to make a great start and work your way around using what you now know. Don't forget the basic language skills that you have learned in this book. If you don't know how to say something, ask, use context clues, describe it using the language that you know, and you will eventually find the answer.

Don't worry about looking silly and just do your best to learn from the mistakes you make! Keep a journal to write about your experiences and the new things that you are learning every day. Though it's not always easy and sometimes rather frustrating, traveling abroad is one of the most rewarding experiences you will have. I hope this book has prepared you well and wish you many exciting and fulfilling adventures in your travels!

To your success,

Dagny Taggart

>> Get The Full Spanish Online Course With Audio Lessons <<

If you truly want to learn Spanish 300% FASTER, then hear this out.

I've partnered with the most revolutionary language teachers to bring you the very best Spanish online course I've ever seen. It's a mind-blowing program specifically created for language hackers such as ourselves. It will allow you learn Spanish 3x faster, straight from the comfort of your own home, office, or wherever you may be. It's like having an unfair advantage!

The Online Course consists of:

+ 185 Built-In Lessons
+ 98 Interactive Audio Lessons
+ 24/7 Support to Keep You Going

The program is extremely engaging, fun, and easy-going. You won't even notice you are learning a complex foreign language from scratch. And before you realize it, by the time you go through all the lessons you will officially become a truly solid Spanish speaker.

Old classrooms are a thing of the past. It's time for a language revolution.

If you'd like to go the extra mile, follow the link below and let the revolution begin

>> http://www.bitly.com/Spanish-Course <<

CHECK OUT THE COURSE »

PS: Can I Ask You a Quick Favor?

If you liked the book, please leave a nice review on Amazon! I'd absolutely love to hear your feedback. Every time I read your reviews... you make me smile. Please go to Amazon right now (following the link below), and write down a quick line sharing with me your experience. I personally read ALL the reviews there, and I'm thrilled to hear your feedback and honest motivation. It's what keeps me going, and helps me improve everyday =)

Go to Amazon by following the link below and write a quick review!

>> http://www.amazon.com/Spanish-Ultimate-Learning-Language-Communication-ebook/dp/B00JYM6XSS/ <<

***

ONCE YOU'RE BACK,
FLIP THE PAGE!
BONUS CHAPTER AHEAD
=)

Preview Of "Spanish *For Tourists - The Most Essential Spanish Guide to Travel Abroad, Meet People & Find Your Way Around - All While Speaking Perfect Spanish!"*

Introduction
Prepare Yourself, We're About to Depart!

To truly learn a language one must commit to hours of studying and in the best scenario travel to the country where that language is spoken. However, what if you want to just prepare to go to that country in order to survive and get by with what you need? This book is the survival guide just for this purpose! It is set up in a simple way so that you can quickly find what you need specific to your situation. We will offer language that covers topics including travel, business, everyday life, social events, meeting new people, and introducing yourself to name a few. Each chapter will provide examples and opportunities to practice and test the knowledge that you have obtained. After each section, there are practice questions and the answers immediately follow them. So don't worry if you get stuck on one. Just try your best, use context clues if you don't know a word, then check the answer. You will notice some vocabulary and phrases are repeated throughout the book. Language repetition is key in retaining new vocabulary!

When you finish with this book you will be ready to travel and enjoy the Spanish-speaking country of your choice. We also include a bonus at the end of the book recommending ten of the best places to visit along with some useful slang to help you sound like a native in Spain (or at least like a very knowledgeable gringa or gringo.) Along with this, we offer several language learning web sites to further your language development. Remember to have an open mind and realize that languages do not translate word for word but rather through ideas. Also, don't worry about making mistakes in the language because they just provide opportunities for you to learn more! Remember to have fun and you will have a wonderful language learning journey. Let's get started!

Building a Foundation in Spanish

The introduction will give you a general description of Spanish-speaking culture, pronunciation, grammatical structure, and lastly provide you with useful words and phrases in Spanish. Understanding culture is such an important part of being able to communicate with others. Language is definitely more than just verbal. Facial expressions, gestures, body language, etc. all contribute to communication. Along with this we will give you a base for pronunciation and grammatical structure. Correct pronunciation is essential to language learning. Some letters in Spanish are pronounced in a very different way than in English. I will provide you with a pronunciation guide for this. You also can use many of the language websites we suggest at the end of the book or google translate to help you pronounce the words in Spanish. Lastly, understanding the order and structure of the language is necessary to make sure you are communicating clearly. Using these three topics, this chapter will give you a base to get started learning the Spanish language!

Culturally Speaking

Every Spanish-speaking country has a slightly different culture but there are some similarities that you will find throughout. A common thread I have found throughout Latin America is the hospitality. If you go to someone's home they are most likely going to offer you something to drink, eat, and maybe even give you some fruit or vegetables to take home. You feel incredibly welcome, like you are in your own home. The importance of family and closeness of friends and neighbors is another common characteristic. I find in American culture individual achievement is most important. In contrast, in Latin-American cultures helping each other, whether it be family, friends or neighbors, is priority. You sometimes will find that within a neighborhood, the neighbors live as if they were family, in and out of each other's houses, in constant contact with each other. Our culture of being holed up in our home and having minimum contact with neighbors is unheard of. Below are the categories of culture that we will discuss.

- *-The 'Mañana' Concept*
- *-Honesty is the Best Policy*
- *-The Melting Pot of Latin America*
- *-Yeah! Another religious Holiday!*
- *-Gesticular Differentiation*
- *-Learning to Live in Lack of Luxury*

The 'Mañana' Concept

You will also find that the Latin American concept of time is quite different. The culture is generally more relaxed than ours when it comes to time. When it comes to services in almost any realm, you will have to be reminded that patience is a virtue. If a party is scheduled at 7pm, you might be expected to show up at 9. If a company is scheduled to install the internet in your apartment on Thursday at 3pm, you can expect them the following Wednesday around 6pm. In many countries, it is also true that businesses will close down in the afternoon from two to four hours for lunch. People also have a long lunch hour and will go home to **'almorzar'** (to eat lunch) and take a nap before going back to work. These usually means they will end up getting off work around 7 or 8 instead of 5.

Honesty is the Best Policy

Along with this, you will notice that honesty truly is the best policy in most Latin-American cultures. So don't feel bad if someone tells you it seems that you are a little more **gordito** (chubby) since the last time they saw you or if your hair just seems incredibly dry and you need a deep conditioning treatment. I believe their opinion is that they are helping out the other person by commenting on their flaws so he or she can become a better person. Just take it with a grain of salt, nod, and smile. I think it is always helpful to be prepared for these kinds of moments so that you do not get offended by the other party. It is common for everyone to be involved in each other's lives and try to help the other even if you don't feel like you need it. Again don't take offense, smile, and move on.

The Melting Pot of Latin America

The majority of Spanish-speaking countries are countries that have been colonized and **conquistado** (conquered) by another country (Spain). This typically means that these countries include a plethora of people: the Indigenous people of the country, Europeans, and Africans. This results in a culture that draws from many different backgrounds. Catholicism is the most common religion that often will have sprinkles of indigenous and African religious customs mixed in. Religion typically plays a very important role in the culture. You will often hear God mentioned in daily conversation. When saying, **'Hasta luego'** (See you later) you will hear the other say, **'Si Dios quiere,'** (God-willing). The idea is that we don't have control but rather God is the commanding, omniscient character in our lives.

Yeah! Another religious Holiday!

Another way that the religion affects the culture is the impressive quantity of holidays. If you happen to work in one of these countries you will enjoy many days off and when you ask the natives the reason for the holiday, many times they are not really sure, probably celebrating a saint, they will say. Celebrations and holidays do play a large role in Spanish-speaking cultures. From the running of the bulls in Spain to the celebration of **Carnaval** throughout Latin America. There are many culturally colorful celebrations and holidays to be enjoyed.

Gesticular Differentiation

Another important aspect to mention is the different types of gestures, facial expressions, and body languages used in these cultures. In general, I have found that people are more animated and use their hands much more to gesture when talking. It is common to see two people in the street that appear to be having a heated argument and then you later find out they were just discussing the recent change in the weather. Something interesting I have noticed as well is that in some countries the people will point with their lips instead of their fingers. When greeting, many people also will kiss once on the cheek (twice in Spain starting with the left one). Men with other men typically will shake hands or hug if they are close. You will find people are generally much more affectionate, touchier, and may not respect the personal space that we are so used to having.

Learning to live in lack of luxury

Lastly, something I have found travelling to almost any other country is that we as Americans are incredibly spoiled. In no other country will you likely find the comforts and luxuries that we have in our country. And they truly are luxuries. You may find that you have to take cold showers, don't have constant access to the internet, the hotel bed is hard as a rock, or in general the area is not as clean as you are used to. You will have to remember to have an open mind, don't whine, and be incredibly thankful for what you do have.

Chapter 1
Basic Pronunciation Guidelines

I have provided two charts to help explain the pronunciation in Spanish, one containing the vowel sounds and the other the consonants. As far as vowel pronunciation goes, Spanish is much simpler than English. Spanish has five vowels that do not change. So you can always depend on the 'a' sounding like 'ah' and the 'i' sounding like 'ee', etc. English, on the other hand, also has five vowels but these five vowels can make up to 27 different sounds. Be thankful if you do not have to learn English as a second language. I sure am! Use these charts to help you pronounce the words throughout the books. Remember that you can also use the language websites at the end of the book or google translate. Just type the word in Spanish and click on the speaker icon to hear the pronunciation.

Vowel Pronunciation Chart

Vowel	How to say the letter	How to pronounce it in a word	As in...
a	Ah	Ah	T<u>o</u>p
e	A	A	B<u>a</u>ke
i	Ee	Ee	M<u>ea</u>t
o	Oh	Oh	B<u>oa</u>t
u	Oo	Oo	C<u>oo</u>k

Consonant Pronunciation Chart

Consonant	How to say the letter	How to pronounce it in a word	As in...
b	bay	similar to English b	
c	say	k after *a, o,* or *u* s after *e* or *i*	<u>c</u>oke <u>s</u>it
ch	chay	ch	<u>Ch</u>eck
d	day	a soft d (place your tongue at the back of your upper teeth)	
f	effay	f	
g	hay	h before i or e	<u>h</u>at

		g before a, o, u	get
h	achay	silent	
j	hota	h	Him
k	kah	k	Karate
l	ellay	like English l with tongue raised to roof of mouth	
ll	doblay ellay	y	Yellow
m	emmay	m	
n	ennay	n	
ñ	enyay	ny	Canyon
p	pay	like English p but you don't aspirate	
q	koo	k (q is always followed by u but the u is silent) Ex: quemar = kaymar	
r	eray	* at the beginning of a word you must roll your r's by vibrating tongue at roof of mouth * in the middle of a word it sounds like a soft d	
rr	erray	roll your r's as mentioned above	
s	essay	Like English s	
t	tay	a soft English t, the tongue touches the back of the upper teeth	
v	vay	like Spanish b	
q	koo	k (q is always followed by u but the u is silent) Ex: quemar = kaymar	

r	eray	* at the beginning of a word you must roll your r's by vibrating tongue at roof of mouth * in the middle of a word it sounds like a soft d	
rr	erray	roll your r's as mentioned above	
s	essay	Like English s	
t	tay	a soft English t, the tongue touches the back of the upper teeth	
v	vay	like Spanish b	
w	doblevay	like English w	
x	equis	*Between vowels and at the end of a word, it sounds like the English *ks*. *At the beginning of a word, it sounds like the letter *s*.	*fo<u>x</u> *<u>s</u>at
y	igriega	like English y	<u>Y</u>ellow
z	sayta	s	<u>S</u>at

Grammar

When discussing the grammar of any foreign language you are learning, it is always important to understand that languages do not translate word for word. They translate as whole ideas instead. You will find some of the differences in the language structure of English and Spanish in this section. It always helps when learning a new language to be able to compare it to your own. In this grammar section I have divided it into eight parts of speech: nouns, pronouns, verbs, adjectives, adverbs, prepositions, conjunctions, and articles. I have also included in this grammar section the categories of word order, diminutives, capitalization and a list of conjugations of commonly used verbs.

   -Parts of Speech
   - Word Order
   - Diminutives
   - Capitalization
   - Verb Conjugation List

Parts of Speech

Nouns

In Spanish the nouns are either feminine or masculine. It has nothing to do with the word's meaning. For example the word *make-up* (***el maquillaje***) is masculine and the word *beard* ***(la barba)*** is feminine.

Ex:

Masculine noun

el libro = the book

Feminine noun

la cosa = the thing

Pronouns

Less Frequent use of Pronouns (I, he, she, we, it, they, etc.): Because of the verb changes mentioned below, you do not have to use pronouns as often. Instead of saying *tú corres*, (you run) you can just say *corres* because we already know that is you who we are talking about from the verb conjugation. In this book, I include both kinds of sentences, with and without the pronouns.

Formal You: There is a formal way to say *you* (Usted usually written Ud.) that is used to show respect to your elders or those in a higher position than you or simply for those whom you don't know well. I used both the informal you (tú) and the formal you (Ud.) throughout this book.

Personal Pronouns

I	Yo
You	Tú
he, she, you (formal)	Él, Ella, Usted (Ud.)
We	Nosotros (masculine) Nosotras (feminine)
You all (informal)	Vosotros (masculine) Vosotras (feminine)
They, you all	Ellos (masculine), Ellas (feminine), Ustedes (Uds.)

¡Ojo! Nosotras is used when it is a group of only females, Nosotros is for only males or a group of mixed gender. The same goes for Ellas/Ellas and Vosotros/Vosotras.

Verbs

Spanish has more verb changes. The verb 'hablar' (to talk) changes 6 times in the present tense. I talk (hablo) you talk (hablas) he or she talks (habla) you all talk (habláis) we talk (hablamos) they or you all talk (hablan). These are called conjugations. For this reason, Spanish also uses personal pronouns much less as I just mentioned. Later in this chapter, I will provide a list of the verb conjugations of the most used verbs in Spanish.

Adjectives

Adjectives describe a noun. The adjectives in Spanish must agree with the gender (feminine or masculine) and the number (singular or plural).

Ex:

El cuaderno blanco --- The white notebook
Las sillas amarillas --- The yellow chairs

Adverbs

Adverbs describe an adjective or a verb. Most of the time, to make an adjective an adverb in Spanish, you take the feminine, singular form and add 'mente' to the end of it. Most adverbs end in 'mente' in Spanish just like most end in 'ly' in English. If an adjective stays the same in the feminine and masculine form, then you just add 'mente.' Such as 'recently.' The adjective is 'reciente' in both masculine and feminine forms, so it changes to 'recientemente' to become an adverb. Of course not all adverbs will end in 'mente' just like not all adverbs in English end in 'ly'.

Ex:

Lento (Slow) to Lentamente (Slowly)

Rápido (Fast) to Rápidamente (Quickly)

Real (Real) to Realmente (Really)

List of Irregular Adverbs

Quite	Bastante
Too/too much	Demasiado
Badly	Mal
A lot	Mucho
Very	Muy
Never	Nunca
Worse	Peor
Little	Poco
Always	Siempre

Prepositions

As I remember learning in elementary school, prepositions are what a squirrel can go… a tree (around, in, over, to, under, etc.) Of course, there are some prepositions that don't fit into that category but it was a good start as an eight year old. In most cases, prepositions in Spanish are used in sentences in a similar way as they are in English. However, most prepositions do not translate easily from English to Spanish or vice versa. Below I have a list of common prepositions.

Common Prepositions

to, at, by means of	A
Before	Antes de
Under	Bajo

Near	Cerca de
With	Con
Against	Contra
Of	De
In front of	Delante de
Inside	Dentro de
Since, from	Desde
After	Después de
Behind	Detrás de
During	Durante
In, on	En
On top of	Encima de
In front of	Enfrente de
Between, among	Entre
Outside of	Fuera de
Toward	Hacia
Until	Hasta
For, in order to	Para
For, by	Por
According to	Según
Without	Sin
Over, about	Sobre
After, behind	Tras

Conjunctions

Conjunctions provide links between words and/or groups of words. What was the conjunction in that previous sentence? You are right! It is 'and/or.' Conjunctions are used in a similar way in both Spanish and English.

So, then	Entonces
Or	O
Either…or	O…o
Neither…nor	No…ni…ni
But	Pero
And	Y

Articles

The Articles in English include 'the', 'a', and 'an.' In Spanish, on the other hand, there are eight different articles. Four of them mean 'the' and four mean 'a' or 'an.' They are said differently according to gender (masculine or feminine) and number (singular or plural). The articles are below and categorized accordingly.

Definite Articles in Spanish (The)

The	Masculine	Feminine
Singular	El	La
Plural	Los	Las

¡Ojo! 'El,' 'la,' 'los,' and 'las' all mean 'the' in English.

Ex:

el libro --- the book.
la cosa --- the thing
los libros --- the books
las cosas --- the things

The articles are much more common in Spanish. Many times when you wouldn't say them in English, you need to say them in Spanish.

Ex: Chocolate is my favorite. = El chocolate es mi favorito.

In English we don't say, 'The chocolate is my favorite...' but in Spanish, you do.

Indefinite Articles in Spanish (A/an)

The	Masculine	Feminine
Singular	Un	Una
Plural	Unos	Unas

¡Ojo! 'Un,' and 'Una,' both mean 'a' in English. And 'Unos,' and 'Unas' both mean 'some.'

Ex:

un libro --- a book.
una cosa --- a thing
unos libros --- some books
unas cosas --- some things

To check out the rest of "*Spanish For Tourists*" *go to Amazon and look for it right now!*

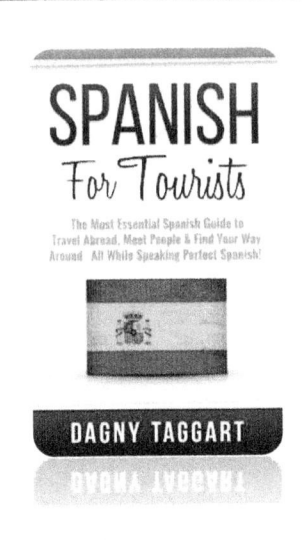

Check Out My Other Books

Are you ready to exceed your limits? Then pick a book from the one below and start learning yet another new language. I can't imagine anything more fun, fulfilling, and exciting!

If you'd like to see the entire list of language guides (there are a ton more!), go to:

>>http://www.amazon.com/Dagny-Taggart/e/B00K54K6CS/<<

About the Author

Dagny Taggart is a language enthusiast and polyglot who travels the world, inevitably picking up more and more languages along the way.

Taggart's true passion became learning languages after she realized the incredible connections with people that it fostered. Now she just can't get enough of it. Although it's taken time, she has acquired vast knowledge on the best and fastest ways to learn languages. But the truth is, she is driven simply by her motive to build exceptional links and bonds with others.

She is inspired everyday by the individuals she meets across the globe. For her, there's simply not anything as rewarding as practicing languages with others because she gets to make friends with people from all that come from a variety of cultures. This, in turn, has broadened her mind and thinking more than she would have ever imagined it could.

Of course, as a result of her constant travels, Taggart has become an expert on planning trips and making the most of time spent out of what she calls her "base" town. She jokes that she's practically at the nomad status now, but she's more content to live that way.

She knows how to live on a manageable budget weather she's in Paris or Phnom Penh. She knows how to seek out the adventures and thrills, no doubt, lying in wait at any city she visits. She knows that reflection on each every experience is significant if she wants to grow as a traveler and student of the world's cultures.

Because of this, Taggart chooses to share her understanding of languages and travel so that others, too, can experience the same life-altering benefits she has.